U0112312

厦门大学百年校庆系列出版物 · 编委会

主　任：张　彦　张　荣

副主任：邓朝晖　李建发　叶世满　邱伟杰

委　员：(按姓氏笔画排序)

王瑞芳　邓朝晖　石慧霞　叶世满　白锡能　朱水涌

江云宝　孙　理　李建发　李智勇　杨　斌　吴立武

邱伟杰　张　荣　张　彦　张建霖　陈　光　陈支平

林　辉　郑文礼　钞晓鸿　洪峻峰　徐进功　蒋东明

韩家淮　赖虹凯　谭绍滨　黎永强　戴　岩

学术总协调人：陈支平

百年校史编纂组　组长：陈支平

百年院系史编纂组　组长：朱水涌

百年组织机构史编纂组　组长：白锡能

百年精神文化系列编纂组　组长：蒋东明

百年学术论著选刊编纂组　组长：洪峻峰

校史资料汇编(第十辑)与学生名录编纂组　组长：石慧霞

厦门大学百年校庆系列出版物
百年学术论著选刊

The Development, Significance and Some Limitations of Hegel's Ethical Teaching

黑格尔的伦理学说

张 颐 著

厦门大学出版社 XIAMEN UNIVERSITY PRESS
国家一级出版社
全国百佳图书出版单位

图书在版编目(CIP)数据

黑格尔的伦理学说＝The Development，Significance and Some Limitations of Hegel's Ethical Teaching:英文/张颐著.—厦门:厦门大学出版社，2021.3
（百年学术论著选刊）
ISBN 978-7-5615-8133-9

Ⅰ.①黑…　Ⅱ.①张…　Ⅲ.①黑格尔(Hegel，Georg Wehelm 1770－1831)－伦理学－研究－英文　Ⅳ.①B516.35②B82

中国版本图书馆 CIP 数据核字(2021)第 048167 号

出　版　人	郑文礼
责任编辑	薛鹏志　林　灿
美术编辑	蒋卓群
技术编辑	朱　楷

出版发行 厦门大学出版社

社　　　址	厦门市软件园二期望海路 39 号
邮政编码	361008
总　　　机	0592-2181111　0592-2181406(传真)
营销中心	0592-2184458　0592-2181365
网　　　址	http://www.xmupress.com
邮　　　箱	xmup@xmupress.com
印　　　刷	厦门兴立通印刷设计有限公司

开本	720 mm×1 000 mm　1/16
印张	11.25
插页	3
版次	2021 年 3 月第 1 版
印次	2021 年 3 月第 1 次印刷
定价	53.00 元

厦门大学出版社
微信二维码

厦门大学出版社
微博二维码

总　序

厦门大学	党委书记　张　彦
	校　长　张　荣

　　2021年4月6日，厦门大学百年华诞。百载风雨，十秩辉煌，这是厦门大学发展的里程碑，继往开来的新起点。全校师生员工和海内外校友满怀深情地期盼这一荣耀时刻的到来。

　　为迎接百年校庆，学校在三年前就启动了"百年校庆系列出版工程"的筹备工作，专门成立"厦门大学百年校庆系列出版物编委会"，加强领导，统一部署。各院系、部门通力合作，众多专家学者和相关单位的工作人员全身心地参与到这项工作之中。同志们满怀高度的责任感和紧迫感，以"提升质量，确保进度，打造精品"为目标，争分夺秒，全力以赴，使这项出版工程得以快速顺利地进行。在这个重要的历史时刻，总结厦大百年奋斗历史，阐扬百年厦大"四种精神"，抒写厦大为伟大祖国所做出的突出贡献，激发厦大人的自豪感和使命感，无疑是献给百岁厦大最好的生日礼物。

　　"百年校庆系列出版工程"包括组织编撰百年校史、百年组织机构史、百年院系史、百年精神文化、百年学术论著选刊、校史资料与学生名录……有多个系列近150种图书将与广大读者见面。从图书规模、涉及领域、参编人员等角度看，此项出版工程极为浩大。这些出版物的问世，将为学校留下大量珍贵的历史资料，为学校深入开展校史教育提供丰富生动的素材，也将为弘扬厦门大学"自强不息，止于至善"校训精神注入时代的新鲜血液，帮助人们透过"中国最美大学校园"

的山海空间和历史回响，更加清晰地理解厦门大学在中国发展进程中发挥的独特作用、扮演的重要角色，领略"南方之强"的文化与精神魅力。

百年校庆系列出版物将多方呈现百年厦大的精彩历史画卷。这些凝聚全校师生员工心血的出版物，让我们感受到厦大人弦歌不辍的精神风貌。图文并茂的《厦门大学百年校史》，穿越历史长廊，带领我们聆听厦大不平凡百年岁月的历史足音。《为吾国放一异彩——厦门大学与伟大祖国》浓墨重彩地记述厦门大学与全国34个省级行政区以及福建省九市一区一县血浓于水的校地情缘，从中可以读出厦门大学在中华民族伟大复兴征程中留下的深深烙印。参与面最广的"厦门大学百年院系史系列"、《厦门大学百年组织机构史》，共有30多个学院和直属单位参与编写，通过对厦门大学各学院和组织机构发展脉络、演变轨迹的细致梳理，深入介绍厦门大学的党建工作、学科建设、人才培养、组织管理、社会服务等方面的发展历程，展示办学成就，彰显办学特色。《厦门大学校史资料选编（1992—2017）》和《南强之星——厦门大学学生名录（2010—2019）》，连同已经出版的同类史料，将较完整、翔实地展现学校发展轨迹，记录下每位厦大学子的荣耀。"厦门大学百年精神文化系列"涵盖人物传记和校园风采两大主题，其中《陈嘉庚传》在搜集大量史料的基础上，以时代精神和崭新视角，生动展现了校主陈嘉庚先生的丰功伟绩。此次推出《林文庆传》《萨本栋传》《汪德耀传》《王亚南传》四部厦门大学老校长传记，是对他们为厦大发展所做出的突出贡献的深切缅怀。厦大校友、红军会计制度创始人、中国共产党金融事业奠基人之一高捷成的传记《我的祖父高捷成》，则是首次全面地介绍这位为中国人民解放事业做出杰出贡献的烈士的事迹。新版《陈景润传》，把这位"最美奋斗者"、"感动中国人物"、令厦大人骄傲的杰出校友、世界著名数学家不平凡的人生再次展现在我们眼前。抒写校园风采的《厦门大学百年建筑》、《厦门大学餐饮百年》、《建南大舞台》、《芙蓉园里尽芳菲》、《我的厦大老师》（百年华诞纪念专辑）、《创新创业厦大人2》、

《志愿之光》、《让建南钟声传响大山深处》、《我的厦大范儿》以及潘维廉的《我在厦大三十年》等，都从不同的角度，引领我们去品读厦门大学的真正内涵，感受厦门大学浓郁的人文精神和科学精神。

此次出版的"厦门大学百年学术论著选刊"，由专家学者精选，重刊一批厦大已故著名学者在校工作期间完成的、具有重要价值的学术论著（包括讲义、未刊印的论著稿本等），目的在于反映和宣传厦门大学百年来的学术成就和贡献，挖掘百年来厦门大学丰厚的历史积淀和传统资源，展示厦门大学的学术底蕴，重建"厦大学派"，为学校"双一流"建设提供学术传统的支撑。学校将把这项工作列入长期规划，在百年校庆时出版第一辑共40种，今后还将陆续出版。

"自强！自强！学海何洋洋！"100年前，陈嘉庚先生于民族危难之际，抱着"教育为立国之本，兴学乃国民天职"的信念，创办了厦门大学这所中国历史上第一所由华侨独资建设的大学。100年来，厦大人秉承"研究高深学术，养成专门人才，阐扬世界文化"的办学宗旨，在实现中华民族伟大复兴的征程上书写自己的精彩篇章。我们相信，当百年校庆的欢庆浪潮归于平静时，这些出版物将会是一串串熠熠生辉的耀眼珍珠，成为记录厦门大学百年奋斗之旅的永恒坐标，成为流淌在人们心中的美好记忆，并将不断激励我们不忘初心继承传统，牢记使命乘风破浪，向着中国特色世界一流大学目标奋勇前行！

张彦　张荣

2020年12月

"厦门大学百年学术论著选刊"
编纂说明

为反映和宣传厦门大学百年来的学术成就和贡献,挖掘厦大学术丰厚的历史积淀和传统资源,为学校"双一流"建设提供学术传统的支撑,"厦门大学百年校庆系列出版物"丛书下设"百年学术论著选刊"系列,以精选、重刊一批我校学者在校期间撰著的、具有重要价值的学术论著。

为此,学校设立"百年学术论著选刊"编纂组,在以校党委书记张彦、校长张荣为主任的"厦门大学百年校庆系列出版物"编委会指导下具体负责这项工作。编纂组组长:洪峻峰;成员:朱水涌、钞晓鸿、高和荣、蒋东明、石慧霞。

鉴于学校将把收集、整理和重刊我校学术论著列入长期规划,今后分辑继续此项工作,"百年学术论著选刊"系列划定选稿范围,内容为百年来在我校工作过的已故学者在校期间撰写或出版的论著,时间以"文革"之前刊印或完成(稿本)为限;确定刊印形式,为原书、原稿影印出版。编纂组于2019年3月向全校各学院、研究院征集选题,同时利用图书馆及图书数据库检索渠道搜索相关文献、查找合适选题。论著的遴选侧重名家名著,同时关注民国时期稀见版本和未刊稿本,包括未曾正式出版的油印本教材。

经学院推荐、文献检索和专家筛选,学校"百年校庆系列出版物"编委会确定了40种入选论著。我们随即展开对论著影印底本的选择和寻访,工作得到了有关图书馆、藏书家的支持和帮助。同时,约请我校各学科相关专业的专家学者分别为各书撰写出版前言,介绍作者生平学术和论著内容价值,揭示其学术史意义及在我校的学术传承。各书前言还将汇编成集,同时出版。

论著选刊工作得到了原著作者的亲属、弟子多方面的支持。部分作品的著作权尚在保护期内,我们也征得其继承人的支持并签约;个别作品无法联系到著作权继承人，我们将公布联系方式，敬请他们与出版社联系。

　　本系列丛书从启动到编成历时两年整。在编纂过程中，学校图书馆、社科处和出版社作为这项工作的协作单位，分别承担了大量的繁杂事务；编纂组秘书黄援生、林灿，以及朱圣明、刘心舜和校图书馆古籍特藏与修复部有关人员，做了许多具体工作。

　　"厦门大学百年学术论著选刊"的编纂，是对我校百年来学术文献资源的一次大规模的搜集、梳理和开发。厦大的学术底蕴和文献资源极为丰厚，第一次选刊难免挂一漏万。经过这次编纂工作的探索，学校今后的分辑整理出版规划将会更加完善。

厦门大学百年学术论著选刊　编纂组

2020 年 12 月

厦门大学百年学术论著选刊（40种）

《中国文学变迁史略》 刘贞晦 著

《教育学原理》 孙贵定 编

《中国古代法理学》 王振先 著

《石遗室诗话》 陈衍 著

《历史哲学》 朱谦之 著

The Development，Significance and Some Limitations of Hegel's Ethical Teaching（《黑格尔的伦理学说》） 张颐 著

《汉文学史纲要》 鲁迅 著

《马哥孛罗游记》 张星烺 译

《闽南游记》 陈万里 著

《厦门音系》 罗常培 著

《教育概论》 庄泽宣 著

《艺术家的难关》 邓以蛰 著

The Li Sao：An Elegy on Encountering Sorrows（《离骚》） 林文庆 译

《老子古微》 缪篆 著

《教育与学校行政原理》 杜佐周 著

《教育社会学》 雷通群 著

《国际私法》 徐砥平 著

《地理学》 王成组 著

《货币银行原理》 陈振骅 著

《文化人类学》 林惠祥 著

《教育之科学研究法》　　钟鲁斋 著

《厦门大学文学院文化陈列所所藏中国明器图谱》　　郑德坤 编著

《因明学》　　虞愚 著

《实用微积分》　　萨本栋、郑曾同、杨龙生 编著

《大学普通化学讲义》　　傅鹰 著

《中国文学史》　　林庚 著

《史学方法实习题汇》　　谷霁光 编

《语言学概要》　　周辨明、黄典诚 译著

《英美法原理》　　[美]阿瑟·古恩 著，陈朝璧 译述

《中国官僚政治研究》　　王亚南 著

《西洋经济思想》　　郭大力 著

《古音学说述略》　　余謇 著

《明清农村社会经济》　　傅衣凌 著

《隋唐五代史纲》　　韩国磐 著

《会计基础知识》　　葛家澍 主编

《文昌鱼》　　金德祥 著

《泛函分析》　　李文清 著

《胚胎学讲义》　　叶毓芬及山东大学胚胎学教研组、汪德耀 编

《浮游生物学概论》　　郑重 著

《海水分析化学》　　陈国珍 主编

前　言

白锡能

《黑格尔的伦理学说》(*The Development, Significance and Some Limitations of Hegel's Ethical Teaching*)是张颐先生1923年提交英国牛津大学以申请哲学博士学位的论文,1925年由商务印书馆出版;次年,张颐先生受聘厦门大学教授后,商务印书馆又出了第二版。《黑格尔的伦理学说》是中国学者研究黑格尔哲学最早问世的一部专著,具有重要的学术价值。该书尤其受到欧美哲学界的重视和高度评价,张颐先生也因此被誉为"东方黑格尔"。

一、作者简介

张颐(1887—1969),字真如,又名唯识,四川省叙永县马岭镇人。张颐6岁开始读书,7岁入私塾。1905年,清王朝在维新运动的压力下,废除了科举制度。1906年,张颐家乡兴办了永宁中学堂,当年张颐考入了该学堂。当时,同盟会党人杨庶堪、朱之洪、向楚等在该校任教。他们极力阐扬三民主义,向学生灌输革命思想。张颐深受他们的影响,遂于1907年加入了同盟会。

1908年夏,张颐偕同盟会员数人负笈赴蓉,以同等学力考入四川省城高等学堂。在校期间,张颐与该校同盟会员并邀其他学校同学组织成立了革命团体勉学会。1909年,张颐又参加杨庶堪、朱之洪、谢持、张培爵等同盟会党人组建的重庆同盟会核心组织乙辛学社,积极参与推翻清政府的革命活动。1911年夏,四川争路事起,各地随即开展了轰轰烈烈的保路爱国斗争。重庆同盟会组织乘势策划起义大计,将保路运动转为革命运动,张颐遂毅然辍学,接受组织指派的任务,积极投身于革命斗争。

1911年辛亥革命爆发后,同年11月22日,重庆革命党人举行起义,宣布重庆独立,成立蜀军政府。张培爵被推举为蜀军政府都督。张颐先是担任都督府机要秘书,不久又代理炸弹团团长。成渝军政府合并后,张培爵改任四川民政长。1912年仲夏,张颐奉邀赴蓉,任民政长公署机要秘书,负责草拟和翻译机密函电文稿。

张颐早年憧憬自由,向往民主,怀有出洋留学、探求真理之愿,故在从事革命活动之余,抓紧时间修习英文及有关科目,为出国留学做准备。1913年,张颐考取四川省公费出国留学项目。同年10月,张颐进入美国密歇根大学,选习哲学。其中,张颐最感兴趣且受益最多的是康德与黑格尔的哲学,他因此而醉心于他们哲学的研究。1917年春,张颐顺利完成本科学业,获得文科学士学位,并随即转入密歇根大学研究院,主修哲学,辅修教育。1918年春,张颐获得哲学硕士学位。之后,他开始撰写博士学位论文《黑格尔伦理学的意义及其局限》("The Significance and Some Limitations of Hegel's Ethics")并于1919年夏天完成论文的写作,经答辩通过,以特优成绩获得哲学博士学位。

1919年秋,张颐获得教育部准许,转学牛津大学,师从史密斯(J. A. Smith)、约阿希姆(H. H. Joachim)等教授,继续西方哲学尤其康德和黑格尔哲学的学习与研究。在此期间,他进一步拓展和深化了对黑格尔伦理学说的研究,取得了突出的学术成就。

1921年春,张颐转学至德国埃尔朗根大学研究班,在德国哲学的故乡更加深入地钻研康德和黑格尔的哲学。1922年夏,张颐移住柏林,参加柏林大学哲学讲演及德国康德学社柏林分社的活动,同时撰写牛津大学的博士学位论文。在柏林期间,张颐多次会晤了著名黑格尔专家拉松(G. Lasson)博士及有关黑格尔研究专家。

1923年春,张颐完成了其学位论文《黑格尔伦理学说的发展、意义与局限》("The Development, Significance and Some Limitations of Hegel's Ethical Teaching"),送交牛津大学审查。经审定和答辩,张颐以优异成绩获得牛津大学哲学博士学位。张颐是获得牛津大学博士学位的第一位中国人。

张颐曾在留美时立志留学十载乃回国服务,故1924年春他便启程回国。回到国内后,张颐乃应北京大学之聘,于是年秋季开始,担任北京大学哲学教授。在北大,张颐讲授"西洋哲学史""德国哲学""康德哲学""黑格尔哲学"等课程。张颐作为早年留学欧美专攻西方哲学特别是康德和黑格尔哲学的著名学者,回到国内登上大学讲坛,首次把地道的康德和黑格尔的哲学带入中国高校哲学系。著名黑格尔专家贺麟先生曾高度评价说:"张真如先生是中国哲学界专门研究西洋古典哲学的先驱……也是中国大学里最早专门地、正规地讲授康德及黑格尔哲学的第一人。"[①]又说，从张颐先生回国在北京大学哲学系"讲授康德和黑格尔哲学时，西方古典哲学才开始真正进入了中国近代大学的哲学系"[②]。

1926年9月，因时局变化，北京已非自由讲学之地，加上当时教师每月薪金只发二成，生活艰难，张颐便应厦门大学创办人陈嘉庚先生的约请，转赴厦门大学担任哲学教授。当时，厦门大学处于初期发展阶段，为了加快学校发展步伐，学校当局重金礼聘著名教授和知名学者。仅1926年，文教商法诸科就聘任了包括鲁迅、林语堂、沈兼士、顾颉刚、张颐、张星烺、庄泽宣等大师和名教授在内的12位教授；1927年又聘任了包括汤用彤、邓以蛰、杨树达、邱椿、李笠、周岸登等名家名师在内的10位教授。加上之前聘任的周辨明、孙贵定、徐声金、陈定谟、陈芝美、艾锷风等名家名师，这时期的厦门大学大文科可谓人才济济、群贤毕至，著名大师和知名教授云集厦大校园，极大提升了厦门大学的学术声望和人才培养质量。在厦大哲学系任教期间，张颐先后担任"论理学""泰西哲学""伦理学史""哲学纲要""康德哲学""黑格尔哲学""德国哲学"等课程的讲授。刚到校的第一个学期，讲授3门课（"论理学""泰西哲学""伦理学史"），每周9课时。他的讲授深受学生的欢迎和好评。张颐教授的到任，有力地推进了厦门大学哲学系西方哲学的研究、教学和人才培养，"康德哲学""黑格尔哲学""德国哲学""西洋伦理学史"等课程正是张颐教授的到来才由他开设起来的。

1927年春，张颐兼任厦门大学文科主任。11月，经林文庆校长推荐，学校董事会决定聘请张颐为副校长。张颐因副校长责任重大，起初未予答应，后经陈嘉庚和陈敬贤两校董力劝，才接受聘任。11月18日，学校发出布告，宣布张颐博士已蒙董事会聘为本校副校长；19日，张颐副校长就职视事。在担任副校长期间，林文庆校长于1928年春和1929年春两次因事滞留南洋，张颐两度作为代理校长主持校务工作。

1928年初，张颐副校长被聘为国民政府教育会议筹备员（会议定于是年5月间在南京召开）。1929年4月，教育部聘请张颐副校长为该部编审处译名委员会委员。

在担任副校长期间，张颐仍兼任文科主任。1928年12月13日，文科同学会邀请文科主任张颐教授在文科同学会第一次学术演讲会上作演讲。张颐教授的演讲题目为"原自由"。演讲历时两个多钟头,对于自由的丰富内涵和实质等问题,作了系统深入的阐述和精到的发挥,听众极为满意。其演讲稿《原自由》后分期刊载在文科同学会出版的《厦门大学文科半月刊》第 1 期(1928年 12 月 30 日出版)和第 2 期(1929 年 1 月 15 日出版)上,1931 年 4 月又收入到《厦门大学演讲集》第一集。1929 年 4 月,为促进文科同学研究学术的兴趣,文科同学会发起组织学术研究会,聘请张颐等文科名教授为指导员。

1929 年 6 月,厦门大学首发年刊。张颐副校长为首期年刊《厦门大学己巳年刊》作序,盛赞陈嘉庚先生独力办学之壮举和厦门大学创办八年来所取得的突出成就:"本校之为陈嘉庚先生独力创办……以一人之力,创办大学,即在欧美亦不多觏,至在吾国,则实破天荒之创举耳。故当其议办之初,一般人士,莫不深致怀疑。而嘉庚先生独能排除众难,毅力不挠,使本校得由孕育而诞生而滋长。迄于今日,建筑设备,逐渐完全,经费源源有继,所有教职员,类皆经验宏富,学有专长,誉遍国中,名闻欧美者……国民政府有鉴于此,曾于去年三月批准立案。"展望未来,"本校前途,实无限量。卅卅年后,或将与英之牛津剑桥、美之哈佛耶鲁、芝加哥诸大学争辉媲"。张颐副校长最后阐明了该刊的宗旨,并勉励教职员和校友继续努力,以成就厦大新的辉煌:"本校过去成绩,虽尚可观,而来日方长,不特本校校董责无旁贷,凡我教职员同人,及先后毕业诸校友,均当共同努力:是刊之出,殆亦将以使吾人览此咸知奋励也夫。"

1929 年 7 月,北平时局稍有好转,张颐先生遂辞去厦门大学职务,重返北京大学担任哲学教授,并于 1930—1933 年兼任北京大学哲学系主任。在此期间,他先后在《大公报》《哲学论丛》上发表了 4 篇关于黑格尔哲学的论文,推动了国内学术界对黑格尔哲学的研究。1935 年夏,张颐先生再赴欧美考察 1年。1936 年回国后,张颐先生应四川大学校长之邀,转任四川大学教授兼文学院院长,次年受教育部委派代理四川大学校长。1939 年秋,应武汉大学校长之邀,张颐先生再转赴武汉大学担任教授。1945 年抗战胜利后,北京大学迁回北平,张颐先生又应邀返回北京大学任教。1948 年,张颐先生因身体不适,回到成都养病。

新中国成立后,张颐先生被聘为四川省文史馆研究员,1955 年又任四川省政协委员。1957 年春,张颐先生又应北大校长马寅初和哲学系主任郑昕的邀请,再次回到北京大学哲学系。从 1957 年起,张颐先生先后连任三届(第二届至第四届)全国政协委员。1969 年,83 岁高龄的张颐先生病情加重,于同年 6

月 23 日逝世于北京。

二、本书的写作与出版

《黑格尔的伦理学说》是张颐先生发表的唯一一部著作,该书系用英文写成并以英文出版。如前所述,该书是张颐先生 1923 年提交牛津大学以申请哲学博士学位的论文。而该论文又是在其留美期间于密歇根大学研究院攻读哲学博士学位时所撰写的博士学位论文的基础上作进一步的拓展研究和深入思考之后撰写而成的。

尚在密歇根大学本科阶段,张颐于 1916—1917 学年参加了温莱(R. W. Wenley)教授主讲的"康德与黑格尔哲学及其对于英美哲学之影响"进修班,对康德和黑格尔哲学特别感兴趣并深受影响,尤其醉心于黑格尔哲学的研究。1917 年转入研究生阶段后,张颐又在欧洲大陆有关哲学、黑格尔哲学和形而上学的三个研究班中获得很多教益。1918 年夏,在获得哲学硕士学位之后,张颐与温莱教授商量,决定以黑格尔的伦理学为主题撰写博士学位论文。张颐在《黑格尔的伦理学说》"前言"中写道:"我于 1918 年在密西根大学开始写作《黑格尔的伦理学说》这篇论文,当时是以《黑格尔伦理学的意义及其局限》的题目呈交的。1919 年 6 月完成了一部分,并以此作为密西根大学的哲学博士学位论文。"③

1919 年 10 月,张颐到达牛津大学后,原本打算采用另外的题目撰写博士学位论文,但后来听从了史密斯教授的劝告,继续从事黑格尔伦理学说的研究和写作。在这一过程中,一方面,张颐拓展了黑格尔伦理学的研究范围。1919 年 6 月所完成的密歇根大学博士学位论文依据的只是黑格尔的《精神哲学》和《法哲学》中的材料。虽然这两部著作是黑格尔成熟期阐述其伦理学说的主要论著,但仅仅依据这两部著作,未能知晓黑格尔伦理思想的形成和发展过程,对于深入理解和把握黑格尔的伦理学说会有所缺欠。有鉴于此,在牛津大学期间,张颐遂将黑格尔伦理学说的研究范围拓展到黑格尔之前在耶拿和纽伦堡时所写的著作。于是,张颐所完成的牛津大学哲学博士学位论文亦即后来出版的专著,其所依据的材料范围扩大为黑格尔的六部著作:(1)《论自然法的科学研究方法》(写于 1802 年夏,耶拿);(2)《伦理体系》(写于 1802—1803 年,耶拿);(3)《精神现象学》(1807 年出版,耶拿);(4)《哲学入门》(写于

1808—1811年,纽伦堡);(5)《精神哲学》(1817年出版,海德堡);(6)《法哲学》(1821年出版,柏林)。这样,就可以清楚地勾勒出黑格尔伦理学说从早期到成熟时期的发展过程,进而达到对黑格尔伦理学说的更为深刻的把握和更为透彻的阐述。

另一方面,在对黑格尔伦理思想的形成和发展过程的梳理并进一步对其伦理学说的系统深入研究的基础上,张颐对1919年6月提交的论文作了大幅度的修改和补充,增加了许多新的内容。其中,"第一、二、三章和第四章一部分是新增加的……第四章的一部分和第九章从前一本书的第一、三、五章吸收了某些材料,但是经过改动和充分的论证,这些章节已呈现出完全不同的性质。第六、七、八章的内容在前本书的第三、四章中曾作过相应的讨论,但它们现在从形式到内容都完全是另一回事"④。全书只有第五章与前一篇论文的第二章基本上是一样的,只是作了某些文字的修改。

张颐1924年回国后,是年在《学艺》杂志上分四期(第六卷第一、二、三号及第六号)发表了其牛津大学的博士论文。1925年5月,该书由商务印书馆出版,书名为:*Hegel's Ethical Teaching:Its Development,Significance and Limitations*(《黑格尔的伦理学说:其发展、意义与局限》);1926年10月,商务印书馆又出版了该书第二版,书名改回原来博士论文的名称:*The Development,Significance and Some Limitations of Hegel's Ethical Teaching*(《黑格尔伦理学说的发展、意义与局限》)。

张颐这部著作的出版,颇受欧美哲学家的重视和好评,在西方学术界引起了较大的反响。牛津大学史密斯教授为该书作序,认为"张博士关于黑格尔伦理学说的著作是他对有关材料进行耐心而透彻研究的成果,也是对我们能自由使用的有意义的论据及其相互联系深思熟虑的成果"。史密斯教授还充分肯定了该书对黑格尔伦理学说所作评价是"非常公正"的,认为该书"必定会受到许多人的欢迎"。史密斯教授特别指出了张颐博士在讨论黑格尔关于家庭及其与国家关系的观点时,不仅批评了黑格尔,而且考察了一般西方思想与制度所依据的偏见,并认为张颐博士的这些反思在某些方面引入了生活所经历的教训,而"通过这些教训的引入,哲学进展了;由于采用了这种方法,张博士对哲学的进展作出了贡献"⑤。在该书出版后,剑桥大学三一学院前教侣、南威尔士大学哲学教授墨铿惹(J. S. Mackenzie)于1926年在芝加哥大学的《国际伦理学杂志》上发表了书评,对该书给予了很高的评价,认为"是书搜述详尽,评解新颖,允为当世赫学可贵之要籍"。他认为,该书哀集黑格尔各种著作中的伦理学说,疏通其脉络,融会其旨趣,深入浅出,将晦涩变为明晰,"不惟其伦理学说之新境陡辟,既全系统亦眉目犁然";并认为一般人对黑格尔哲学"每有误解其意甚或讹传其义者",而"张氏此作,可谓……能举此种谬误,摧陷而廓清之者矣"。为此,他明确表示可以"深信不疑"为读者力荐此作。⑥1927年,德国习尔熙(E. Hirsch)教授在莱比锡大学的一份杂志上也发表了书评,尽管他不是哲学领域的专家,但对该书也表示了欢迎和肯定。1928年,以编辑出版《黑格尔全集》而闻名的黑格尔专家拉松博士在柏林出版的《康德研究》第33卷上对该书作了评论,完全同意张颐对于黑格尔哲学所作的陈述和疏解,并认为该书对于黑格尔的评价,较许多德国作者更为公允。欧美尚有一些教授,虽未发表书评,但给作者来函表示欢迎。这其中就包括英国哲学史大家费歇尔(K. Fischer)教授,他于1926年给张颐写信,对该书的出版表达了热情的欢迎,并申明其所以没有撰写书评,乃是由于近期忙于管理事务而无暇细读的缘故。国内研究西方哲学东渐史的知名学者黄见德教授在谈到张颐先生这部著作在国外的反响时说道:"一部中国学者研究黑格尔的著作,这样受到国际哲学界的广泛关注与积极评价,这在西方哲学东渐史上是极其罕见的。"⑦

作为牛津大学的博士学位论文,张颐先生的这部著作是用英文撰写的,商务印书馆也是按英文原著出版和再版的。该书长期以来一直未有中文译本问世,这在一定程度上影响了该书在国内的传播。在贺麟先生的提议和推动下,四川省社会科学院张桂权研究员于1988年根据商务印书馆1926年第二版完成了张颐先生这部重要著作的中文翻译工作,该译本于2000年收入在侯成亚、张桂权、张文达编译的《张颐论黑格尔》一书中,由四川大学出版社出版。《张颐论黑格尔》除载有张颐先生的《黑格尔的伦理学说》外,还收入张颐先生讨论黑格尔哲学的4篇论文及1篇介绍美国圣路易哲学运动的文章,同时附有张颐之子张文达先生撰写的"张颐传略"和"张颐年谱"。

三、本书的基本内容和学术价值

张颐先生的《黑格尔的伦理学说》,顾名思义,是以黑格尔的伦理学说为研究对象的。但是,他不是从通常理解的狭义伦理学的视角去理解和梳理黑格尔的伦理观点,而是忠实于黑格尔的学说,把研究对象置于黑格尔的哲学体系中,按照黑格尔的思路,将其伦理学说与其关于经济学、政治学、法学、思辨哲学等方面的论述有机结合起来加以系统深入的研究,并从黑格尔哲学思想的形成和发展的历程中去探讨和把握其伦理学说的形成和发展。通过纵横两个维度的详细考察和透彻研究,该书全面深刻地阐述了黑格尔伦理学说从早期到成熟期的发展过程,透彻而客观地叙述了黑格尔各个时期的伦理观点,并从中归纳出黑格尔伦理学说的一般特征,探讨了黑格尔伦理学说的形而上学基础,作者以批判的态度指出了黑格尔伦理学说存在的困难和局限,提出了自己的独立见解,对黑格尔伦理学说的意义作出了较公正的评价。

西方古典哲学是以论证自由和善的目标为其终极价值的追求,所以从古希腊哲学到近代西方哲学,许多哲学家都著有以"伦理学"或相关名称命名的以伦理道德为研究主题的著作,如亚里士多德的《尼各马可伦理学》、斯宾诺莎的《伦理学》和康德的《实践理性批判》。张颐先生则注意到黑格尔从未使用"伦理学"或"道德学"命名过其重要著作。虽然黑格尔早期有一部著作名叫《伦理体系》,但这部著作在黑格尔在世时既没有写完也没有出版,直到半个多世纪后才由后人首次出版。尽管黑格尔未将其重要著作起名为"伦理学",张颐先生仍认为,"黑格尔有伦理学说",而且"论述是如此透彻和有独创性"。[8]只是,"黑格尔的伦理学说不是呈现为一个单一的部分,而是混合者或分散于心理学、经济学、政治学、法学、美学、宗教学和思辨哲学的论述中"。[9]因为对黑格尔来说,"对伦理学的基本论述不能够与对生活的其他部分的论述分离开"。[10]这就是说,人的自我实现,一方面必须以自然存在和社会合作为基础,另一方面又要达到与绝对精神的某种统一。因此,伦理学一方面必须深入自然的和社会的生活,另一方面又必须超出有限的范围而进入审美、纯思的绝对精神王国。显然,张颐先生对黑格尔的哲学理念和思维进路有着深刻的理解和精到的把握。不过,张颐先生也提出,为方便起见,我们在论述伦理学时,可以把注意力集中在生活的伦理方面,而对其他相关的方面只作附带的讨论;当然,形而上学与伦理学之间的关系问题需要多花一些笔墨,因为伦理学必须建立在形而上学的坚实的基础上。基于上述见解,张颐先生的这部著作就把研究的对象范围限定在前面提到的黑格尔的六部著作上,而在研究的内容上,尽管涉及黑格尔哲学的众多领域,但其主线是社会生活的伦理方面,重点又是黑格尔关于客观精神(特别是《精神哲学》和《法哲学》中的客观精神)的伦理学说,同时设有专章讨论黑格尔伦理学说的形而上学基础问题。

《黑格尔的伦理学说》共分为九章。从结构上说,这九章可分别归为三个部分。第一部分是第一章至第五章,主要是系统梳理黑格尔从1802年到1921年在其六部著作中所阐述的伦理学说,并用晓畅明白的语言加以表达;其中,对黑格尔的哲学体系作了简要的概述,并说明伦理学在其体系中所占的地位和《法哲学》是怎样逐渐扩展成为单独一部著作的。第二部分仅为第六章,主要是概括黑格尔伦理学说的一般特征,追溯黑格尔伦理观点的发生过程和形成原因,分析黑格尔伦理学说存在的困难,消除一些人对黑格尔伦理学说的误解。第三部分包括第七至第九章,主要是对黑格尔伦理学说的意义作出批判性的评价,指出其局限。这部分的内容包括:强调伦理理念的客观表现的意义和伦理行为中的客观准则的重要性;讨论伦理学理论的形而上学基础的必要性,考察黑格尔对他的形而上学原则的应用;讨论黑格尔伦理学说中的某些特殊问题,并提出自己的不同看法。

　　张颐先生的《黑格尔的伦理学说》是我国最早出版的黑格尔研究专著,也是国际上最早出版的专门论述黑格尔伦理学说的专著之一,在黑格尔的伦理学说乃至黑格尔哲学的研究史上具有重要的学术价值。在张颐的著作出版前,国外已出版的专门论述黑格尔伦理学说的专著就只有开普敦大学的雷伯恩(Hugh Adam Reyburn)教授于1921年在牛津出版的《黑格尔的伦理理论:法哲学研究》(*The Ethical Theory of Hegel*:*A Study of the Philosophy of Right*)。但该书只是对黑格尔的《精神哲学》和《法哲学》的研究,未考察黑格尔之前的其他有关著作;而且据作者所说,该书主要是对黑格尔伦理学说的解读和说明,以便使黑格尔的观点更容易理解,因此书中的批评已被减少到最低限度。而张颐先生的著作所提供的是鸟瞰黑格尔的伦理学说从早期到成熟期的全部发展,并对黑格尔的学说作出批评性的评价,而不只是单纯的解释。除了雷伯恩教授的这部专著外,国外就没有其他专门论述黑格尔伦理学说的著作了,有的只是在相关著作中对这一内容有所涉及而已,而这与专门且系统地论述黑格尔的伦理学说是不一样的。张颐先生在查证了之前有关黑格尔伦理学说的研究著作的出版情况后,总结道:“就我所知,到目前为止,还没有专门论述贯穿在黑格尔的各种著作中的伦理学说和对其价值作出批评性评价的著作。”[①]因此,也可以说,即便在国外,张颐的著作也是第一部专门论述贯穿在黑格尔的各种著作中的伦理学说并对其作出批评性评价的著作。

　　在张颐先生的著作之后,国外出版的专门论述黑格尔伦理学说的著作也

9

没有几部。稍早一点的为爱丁堡大学沃尔什(W. H. Walsh)教授于1969年出版的《黑格尔学派的伦理学》(Hegelian Ethics),但其不仅篇幅不及张颐的著作,而且不是专门讨论黑格尔的伦理学,因此对于黑格尔伦理学的论述也就更简略了。稍近一点的为当代著名德国古典哲学研究专家、斯坦福大学哲学系荣休讲席教授伍德(Allen W. Wood)于1990年出版的《黑格尔的伦理思想》(Hegelian Ethics),该书获得很高的评价,被认为是对于黑格尔伦理学的最为重要的研究。

在国内,虽然黑格尔哲学的传入在19世纪末20世纪初就开始了,但在20世纪30年代之前,黑格尔哲学的传播和研究尚处在起步阶段,在当时特定的时代背景下,学术界在这方面的声音相当沉寂,远不及康德哲学的传播和研究。张颐1924年刚回到国内时就感受到了这种氛围:"所遇友朋皆侈谈康德,不及黑格尔,竞言认识论,蔑视形而上学。"⑫在那个时期,学术界很少发表讲述黑格尔的文章。在张颐的著作出版之前,主要是一些西洋通史或传记类作品等相关的著作和文章中包含着关于黑格尔的简单介绍,专门论述黑格尔的文章也就只有3篇:最早一篇为马君武的《唯心派巨子黑智儿学说》,1903年发表在《新民丛报》第27号;其次是严复的《述黑格儿唯心论》,1906年发表在《寰球学生报》第2期;第三篇是瞿世英的《黑格尔》,1921年发表在《时事新报》上。再有就是张颐1924年分期发表在《学艺》杂志上的牛津大学博士学位论文了。至于专门论述黑格尔的著作,在此之前尚为空白;而且,在此之后也没有专门论述黑格尔伦理学说的系统性著作。不过,从20世纪30年代起,国内黑格尔哲学的研究和传播迅速兴盛起来,仅30年代就翻译和撰写出版了10来部黑格尔的原著和研究著作,有关黑格尔哲学的论文更是有上百篇之多。可以说,张颐这部著作的出版,对推动国内黑格尔哲学的传播和研究,起到了重要的作用。由此可见,张颐的《黑格尔的伦理学说》一书的出版,在国内黑格尔哲学特别是其伦理学的研究史上具有更加重要的意义。著名黑格尔专家张世英教授曾高度评价张颐先生的这部著作,称其为研究黑格尔的"经典之作"。作为一部备受国内外黑格尔专家盛赞和推崇的学术著作,对于我们今天了解黑格尔哲学的形成和发展,系统深入地研究黑格尔的伦理学说,仍具有重要的参考价值。

注释：

①贺麟：《卷首献词》，《哲学评论》1947年第10卷特刊，转引自侯成亚、张桂权、张文达编译：《张颐论黑格尔》，成都：四川大学出版社，2000年，第243页。

②贺麟：《五十年来的中国哲学》，沈阳：辽宁教育出版社，1989年，第96页。

③张颐：《黑格尔的伦理学说》，侯成亚、张桂权、张文达编译：《张颐论黑格尔》，成都：四川大学出版社，2000年，第9页。

④张颐：《黑格尔的伦理学说》，侯成亚、张桂权、张文达编译：《张颐论黑格尔》，成都：四川大学出版社，2000年，第9页。

⑤[英]史密斯：《张颐著〈黑格尔的伦理学说〉序》，侯成亚、张桂权、张文达编译：《张颐论黑格尔》，成都：四川大学出版社，2000年，第8页。

⑥[英]麦铿籍：《读张颐博士赫氏伦理探究》，《厦大周刊》1929年第200~201期合刊，第11~12页。

⑦黄见德：《西方哲学东渐史：上卷》，北京：人民出版社，2006年，第364页。

⑧张颐：《黑格尔的伦理学说》，侯成亚、张桂权、张文达编译：《张颐论黑格尔》，成都：四川大学出版社，2000年，第11页。

⑨张颐：《黑格尔的伦理学说》，侯成亚、张桂权、张文达编译：《张颐论黑格尔》，成都：四川大学出版社，2000年，第11页。

⑩张颐：《黑格尔的伦理学说》，侯成亚、张桂权、张文达编译：《张颐论黑格尔》，成都：四川大学出版社，2000年，第11页。

⑪张颐：《黑格尔的伦理学说》，侯成亚、张桂权、张文达编译：《张颐论黑格尔》，成都：四川大学出版社，2000年，第10页。

⑫张颐：《读克洛那、张君劢、瞿菊农、贺麟诸先生黑格尔逝世百年纪念论文》，侯成亚、张桂权、张文达编译：《张颐论黑格尔》，成都：四川大学出版社，2000年，第157页。

作者白锡能，厦门大学马克思主义学院原院长，人文学院哲学系教授。

THE DEVELOPMENT, SIGNIFICANCE
AND SOME LIMITATIONS OF
HEGEL'S ETHICAL TEACHING

张颐著 *The Development, Significance and Some Limitations of Hegel's Ethical Teaching* （《黑格尔的伦理学说》），影印底本：商务印书馆 1926年10月再版，原书尺寸：158mm×228mm。

THE DEVELOPMENT, SIGNIFICANCE
AND SOME LIMITATIONS OF
HEGEL'S ETHICAL TEACHING

THE DEVELOPMENT, SIGNIFICANCE
AND SOME LIMITATIONS OF
HEGEL'S ETHICAL TEACHING

BY

W. S. CHANG, Ph. D. (Mich.), D. Phil. (Oxon.)

PROFESSOR OF PHILOSOPHY AND EDUCATION IN THE NATIONAL UNIVERSITY OF PEKING

PUBLISHED UNDER THE AUSPICES OF
THE CHINA SOCIETY OF ARTS AND SCIENCE

THE COMMERCIAL PRESS, LIMITED
SHANGHAI, CHINA
1926

TO THE MEMORY

OF

MY MOTHER

WHO PASSED AWAY

WHEN I ARRIVED

IN

THE UNITED STATES OF AMERICA

THIS VOLUME IS DEDICATED

PREFACE

Dr. Chang's work on the ethical doctrines of Hegel is the fruit of patient and thorough study of the relevant materials and of prolonged meditation upon the significance and inter-connection of the evidence at our command. He has informed his mind well concerning the background and surroundings of Hegel's philosophizing, and has a just sense of its place in the age-long history of Western Philosophy. The result is a presentment of one important side of it which is at once sympathetic and discriminating. He realizes the breadth and depth of the foundations upon which Hegel based his ethical doctrines and the magnificent sweep of his speculative vision ; at the same time he sees and emphasizes the closeness of its contact with ordinary experience and workaday problems. Too often Hegel has been represented as an eagle " sailing with supreme dominion in the azure deep of air," and too little acknowledgment has been made of his practical wisdom and his sturdy, and to tell the truth, often pedestrian common sense. This more earthly quality of the master Dr. Chang justly appreciates, indicating both its strength and its weakness, distinguishing between that in its content which is " for all time " and that which is due to the special circumstances of its origin, and is almost fortuitous and is certainly moribund, if not already dead. The justness of the appraisal is remarkable as coming from one who has necessarily approached it from a distance unusually remote, and the achievement is not only highly creditable to Dr. Chang's industry and insight, but must be welcome to all those who believe in the universality of the appeal which such a philosophy makes to the mind of man. The work is calculated to promote that mutual understanding between East and West which all must desire to see developed and confirmed.

Of special interest is Dr. Chang's discussion of Hegel's views concerning the Family and its relations to and within the State. Here he extends his criticism beyond Hegel and brings under review certain prejudices which underlie Western thought and institutions generally. His reflections on these are expressed with moderation and deserve respectful attention. They call in the lessons of an experience in some relevant respects different from that upon which Hegel drew, and the appeal to them is one which neither Hegel nor we can fairly ignore. It is indeed by such method that Philosophy advances, and in employing it Dr. Chang makes his contribution to that advance.

To his own countrymen this work should prove a helpful instrument in introducing them to the higher levels of Western thought about human conduct and life.

J. A. SMITH.

Magdalen College, Oxford, February, 1924.

PREFACE

This treatise of Hegel's Ethical Teaching was started in 1918 at the University of Michigan and submitted under the title : " The Significance and Some Limitations of Hegel's Ethics," in partial fulfillment of the requirements for the degree of Doctor of Philosophy there, in June, 1919. At that time the work was based on Hegel's " Philosophy of Spirit " and " Philosophy of Right." When I came to Oxford in October, 1919, I proposed to take another subject. Owing to the advice of Professor J. A. Smith I have continued this study. As it appears in the present form, it is based on Hegel's (1) Treatise " *Ueber die wissenschaftlichen Behandlungsarten des Naturrechts*," (2) "*System der Sittlichkeit*," (3) "*Phenomenology of Spirit*," (4) "*Philosophische Propædeutik*," (5) *Philosophy of Spirit*," and (6) "*Philosophy of Right*." Accordingly, Chapters I, II, III, and partly IV are added anew, while Chapter V is almost the same, except for some literary revisions, as Chapter II of my former work. Part of Chapter IV and Chapter IX here draw some material from Chapters I, III, and V there, but through substantial augmentation and alteration they have assumed quite a different character. Chapters VI, VII, and VIII find some corresponding discussions in Chapters III and IV of the former work, but both in form and content they are entirely another thing.

Meanwhile Professor Hugh A. Reyburn has published an admirable work on the same subject. I have read his work carefully, and thank him very much for many points, both in suggestion and corroboration of my views. Had Professor Reyburn's work been a little earlier published the present work would probably not have been undertaken or continued. Yet, like my former work, Professor Reyburn's is professedly a study of Hegel's " Philosophy of Spirit " and " Philosophy of Right," and, as he says in his preface, his work is an endeavor to provide an account which will make Hegel's view more intelligible, and in it criticism has, accordingly, been reduced to a minimum ; whereas what I propose to offer here is a survey of the whole development of Hegel's Ethical

Teaching from his early days up to his maturity, and, further, I have attempted a critical appreciation of the value of his teaching instead of a mere interpretation. So my work may be taken as complementary to that of Professor Reyburn, not as overlapping it.

Among the works of other writers, part of the late Professor G. S. Morris' " Hegel's Philosophy of History " contains a short account of the " Philosophy of Right," while Professor J. M. Sterrett's " The Ethics of Hegel " is a selected translation with an introductory account of the same. Professor W. Wallace in some of his Introductory Essays to his translation of Hegel's " Philosophy of Spirit," drew material from Hegel's " *System der Sittlichkeit*," but that is different from a systematic treatment dealing with Hegel's work. So far as my knowledge goes, a monograph of Hegel's Ethical Teaching throughout his various writings and offering a critical estimate of its value has not been attempted before.

In undertaking this work I am particularly indebted to Professors R. M. Wenley and A. H. Lloyd, of Michigan, and Professor J. A. Smith, of Oxford, for their untiring instruction and valuable advice. Among interpreters and critics of Hegel's Philosophy, I should express my indebtedness to the late Professors W. Wallace, Edward Caird, and K. Fischer, Professors J. B. Baillie and A. S. Pringle-Pattison, Senator B. Croce, and Dr. J. M. E. Mctaggart, while my indebtedness to other writers will be indicated by quotations.

Berlin, April, 1923.   W. S. CHANG.

TABLE OF CONTENTS

PAGE

INTRODUCTION   1

CHAPTER

I. CONCERNING THE SCIENTIFIC MODES OF TREATING NATURAL RIGHT   6

II. THE SYSTEM OF ETHICALITY   14

III. THE PHENOMENOLOGY OF SPIRIT   25

IV. THE PHILOSOPHICAL PROPÆDEUTIC, THE ENCYCLOPÆDIA OF PHILOSOPHICAL SCIENCES AND THE PHILOSOPHY OF RIGHT   43

V. OBJECTIVE SPIRIT AND THE PHILOSOPHY OF RIGHT   50

VI. SOME CHARACTERISTICS AND DIFFICULTIES IN HEGEL'S ETHICAL TEACHING.   72

VII. OBJECTIVE MANIFESTATION AND OBJECTIVE NORM IN HEGEL'S ETHICS.   91

VIII. METAPHYSICAL BACKGROUND AND SOME APPLICATIONS IN HEGEL'S ETHICS   107

IX. SOME SPECIFIC PROBLEMS IN HEGEL'S ETHICAL TEACHING.   121

INTRODUCTION

It is interesting to note that Hegel never bestowed the titles *Ethik* or *Sittenlehre* upon any important work. One of his early writings was entitled " *System der Sittlichkeit*," but this was apparently never finished and remained unpublished till towards the end of the nineteenth century when it was published for the first time by Mollat in 1893. For an outsider, it is not ridiculous to ask if Hegel has any ethical teaching at all. But, nevertheless, he has, and even beginners in his philosophy know that his discussion of Ethics was so thorough and original that it continues to arouse sharp differences of opinion to this day.

Among Hegel's writings every student of his philosophy admits that (1) the Treatise " Concerning Scientific Modes of Treating Natural Right," (2) the " System of Ethicality," [1] (3) the " Phenomenology of Spirit," [2] (4) the " Philosophical Propædeutic," (5) the " Philosophy of Spirit," (6) the " Philosophy of Right," are prominently *ethical*. The " Philosophy of History, of Fine Art, of Religion," and the " History of Philosophy " also have direct or indirect ethical bearings. But the difficulty at once arising here is that Hegel's ethical teaching is, instead of being presented in a single compartment, mixed up with, or scattered in, Psychology, Economics, Politics, Law, Fine Art, Religion, and Speculative Philosophy. For Hegel, however, this is inevitable. To him the fundamental treatment of Ethics cannot be divorced from that of the other departments of life. That is to say, the entire process of human Experience must fall within the reckoning, because human self-realization implies no less. On the one hand, individual man must base himself on natural subsistence and social coöperation. On the other the same individual, as a spiritual being, looks forward to union of some sort with Absolute Spirit — Divine Reason, Oversoul, Heaven, Tao, Brahma, call it what you will. From this standpoint, certainly an Ethical Treatise must, on

1. See Note 1, at end of this Introduction.
2. See Note 2, *ibid.*

1

the one hand, shade over unto the sphere of daily — natural and social — life; and, on the other, reach out into the realm of Absolute Spirit, into æsthetic contemplation, aspirational meditation, and pure speculative activities.

To my mind, Hegel's conception of Ethical life is very comprehensive and admirable, and the justifiability of his method of treatment needs no further advocacy. It has also the advantage of eradicating all mischiefs arising from taking Ethics abstractly or dualistically. But, for the sake of convenience, we may still follow the example set by Aristotle and treat the Ethical aspect of life by itself. It is true that what is ethical cannot possibly be separated from the infra-ethical and the supra-ethical or the pre-ethical and the meta-ethical. But when we are dealing with Ethics, we may concentrate our attention upon this aspect of life. In cases where the infra-ethical and the supra-ethical, or the pre-ethical and the post-ethical, are involved, we may content ourselves with some passing discussions, explaining their bearing upon Ethics, the relationship between them and the latter, etc. So the question here is not a matter of scientific legitimacy, but a matter of convenience. Upon the relation, however, between Metaphysics and Ethics I cannot help dwelling a little longer. For I am quite convinced that a sound Ethical theory must have a solid Metaphysical background, while many writers hold to an entirely opposite standpoint.

Treating Hegel's Ethical Teaching in this spirit, we may concentrate our attention upon the first six works by him mentioned above. Accordingly, the program of the present treatise will contain three chief sections. In the first place the writer proposes to trace out and put in plain terms the Ethical doctrines which Hegel laid down in his various writings from 1802 up to 1821. This will be done in Chapters I to V. In such presentation our philosopher is invited to speak for himself, but here and there explanation and commentary cannot be avoided. Accordingly, in the latter part of Chapter IV, I shall, by way of exposition, give a short sketch of Hegel's philosophical system and try to show what place Ethics holds in the whole system and how the " Philosophy of Right" has come to expand into a separate volume. I insert this short expository account here, for it is a preliminary to Chapter V and will incidentally facilitate the understanding of the latter chapter. On the other hand, the gist of the " Philosophical Propædeutic " by itself is too slight to form a chapter, while the content of the " Objective Spirit " and the " Philosophy of Right " is already too big. These five chapters are exceedingly uneven. But, in the nature of the case, it cannot be otherwise. For Hegel's writings treated there are themselves uneven. We cannot shorten what is long or lengthen what is short.

Secondly, I shall in Chapter VI attempt a general characterization of Hegel's Ethical Teaching, such as his unification of the rational and the real, or the ideal and the actual, his intellectualistic theory of will and freedom, his dialectic exhibition of the self-realization of free will, etc. In this connection I shall also try to trace the genesis of Hegel's position, i. e., recall his inspiration by Hellenic civilization, his own metaphysical standpoint, the temporary situation in his time, etc., so as to make it more intelligible how and why Hegel was led to maintain such an Ethical position. Here the difficulties inherent in his teaching and the usual misunderstandings of it will, so far as possible, be explained, objections to it met, and shortcomings of it pointed out.

Thirdly, I shall attempt a critical appreciation or estimate of the significance of Hegel's Ethical Teaching and try to point out some of its limitations, in short, try to show how far Hegel's Ethical doctrine may be accepted, and in what aspects it is unsatisfactory. This will be done in Chapters VII to IX. Accordingly, in Chapter VII, I shall insist upon the significance of the objective manifestation of the Ethical Idea as it can be illuminated by Hegel's Ethical teaching. This is perhaps superfluous to Western readers, but by Orientals it may be found interesting. In the same chapter I shall also insist upon the importance of an Objective Norm in Ethical conduct. Here the limits of individualism, narrow nationalism, and vague cosmopolitanism will be shown. In Chapter VIII, the necessity of a Metaphysical background for Ethical theory will be discussed at length and Hegel's application of his metaphysical principles will be examined. It is true that we cannot all be metaphysicians. But, nevertheless, we all have *some* metaphysics. One may point to the fact that *very few persons* have been good metaphysicians, but, as supplementary to this, we may also point out that *not everybody* knows really what is good or bad. This point, I hope, will become more clear in the following discourse. Finally, in Chapter IX, I shall discuss some specific problems treated in Hegel's Ethical Teaching. In this respect I should refer the reader to the more or less exhaustive discussions of Professor H. A. Reyburn for complement. Throughout the whole discourse, the main subject at issue is what is properly Ethical. But, as has been mentioned above, Hegel's Ethical discussion is inextricably bound up with other departments of study. Consequently, a total elimination of them from this treatise is almost impossible, and, at times, an appeal and reference to them for explanation and supplement will be found necessary.

Of Hegel's works I have uniformly used Dr. Georg Lasson's edition, except for the " Philosophical Propædeutic," which as yet can be had only in the second edition. Wherever translations are available, I have taken advantage of them, but the original text has always been consulted. In quotations I have adopted Professor Wallace's translation fron Hegel's " Encyclopædia of Philosophical Sciences " without alteration. The same may be said of Professor Baillie's translation of Hegel's "Phenomenology of Spirit." Only sometimes I have found Professor Baillie's translation too free and I have adhered a little more literally to the original text. In such cases I have slightly altered Professor Baillie's rendering, while adopting it in the main. I have derived much assistance from Professor Dyde's translation of Hegel's " Philosophy of Right " and from Professor Sterrett's selected translation of the same, but seldom adopted them without modification.

NOTE 1. For the term "*Sittlichkeit*" no English equivalent is available. Dr. Stirling coined the word " Ethicality." Professor Sterrett in his " Ethics of Hegel " and Professor Dyde in his translation of the " Philosophy of Right " both employ it. Professor J. B. Baillie adopted it in his " Hegal's Logic," but, in his translation of the " Phenomenology of Spirit," prefers the phrase " Ethical Order," which is also the choice of Professor Reyburn in his " Hegel's Ethical Theory." Among other writers Professor Wallace in his translation of Hegel's " Philosophy of Spirit " and Professor G. S. Morris in his " Hegel's Philosophy of

History" called it "Social Ethics" and the "Ethical World," respectively. To my mind, Dr. Stirling's rendering still conveys Hegel's technical meaning best. For in Hegel's view, " *Sittlichkeit* " is the " Idea " or the " Unity of the notion and objectivity " of " Freedom." In other words, it is the living Ethical Spirit which, while actualized in social order, still continues in process of living and actualizing, and has never crystallized. The phrases " Ethical Order " and " Ethical World " express the moment of ' actualized,' but not the moment of living and actualizing, whereas the phrase " Social Ethics " misleadingly suggests that it is only a body of doctrine.

NOTE 2. The term " *Geist* " is also very difficult to translate adequately into English. The word "Spirit" has usually associated with it a religious meaning, while the word " Mind " is insufficient to convey the significance of consciousness or ' experience ' at its higher levels. Professor Baillie in his translation of Hegel's "Phenomenology of Spirit " has from the beginning uniformly rendered the term " *Geist* " by the word "Mind." But when he arrived at the stage of " Spirit," he noticed that here the word " Spirit " seems better than the word " Mind " to render the word " *Geist.* " Now, what I propose to take up in the present treatise all falls within the stage which Hegel calls " *Geist.* " Therefore I have uniformly rendered the term " *Geist* " by the word " Spirit."

NOTE 3. The term " *Stand* " may be rendered by the English words " rank," " estate " or " class." But these are not as general and comprehensive as the German word " *Stand* " and have, further, some association with temporary and local forms of government. I therefore have retained the German term.

CHAPTER I

CONCERNING THE SCIENTIFIC MODES OF TREATING
NATURAL RIGHT

This treatise appeared in the second and third numbers of the *Critical Journal of Philosophy*, which Hegel published jointly with Schelling. It was written in the Summer of 1802 at Jena but the draft was composed in Frankfurt. [1]

In this treatise Hegel's ideal of an ethico-communal life of a nation was philosophically developed; the Greek City-State was conceived as the ideal in actuality. In germ the treatise contains all the forms of " Objective Spirit " as Hegel comprehends it in its totality. Natural right, national economy, and ethics are combined into a whole. In this inter-connection of life, however, the ethical appears as the highest summit. Only later, in the maturer development of his philosophical system, do Art, Religion, and Philosophy advance beyond this realm to the " Absolute Spirit." [2]

At the beginning [3] of the treatise Hegel complains of the common but mistaken practice of treating natural right independently. To him no science can be fundamently separated from Metaphysics. A thorough treatment of any science, therefore, must needs go back to Philosophy where guiding principles are to be found, and the true meaning of a given science is seen for the first time in the perspective of a whole system.

After the discussion in a general way of the method of treatment, Hegel proceeds to criticize the empirical method of Hobbes, while not mentioning his name. [4]

---

1. Cf. Kuno Fischer : Geschichte der Neuern Philosophie, Band VIII, p. 272.
2. Cf. J. B. Baillie : Hegel's Logic, p. 123, and see below, p. 10, note 2.
3. Hegel's Werke, herausgegeben von Lasson, Band VII, pp. 329–334.
4. Cf. K. Fischer : *op. cit.*, p. 273.

6

The empirical method of Hobbes starts with the supposition of a state of nature. In this state of nature human beings behaved like physical entities or units, i. e., atoms. By the instinct of self-preservation the individuals waged a war of all against all. It was only when they became tired of the intolerableness of this state of war, and perhaps also felt the need of socialization, that they came to submit themselves to the dominion of the strongest. A state of right with unity and order was thus established.

The most obvious defect of this view is that human beings are never mere atoms. Consequently the treatment of them in terms of the impulses of self-preservation, socialization, etc., on the analogy of attraction and repulsion in physical science, is illegitimate. The problem of human relations can never be attacked by a physical method of approach.

The state of nature, again, is a fiction. It is reached by abstracting from human beings all that civilization has conferred upon them. [1] There never was such a " naked man " inasmuch as human beings are always found in groups.

Further, there is, in the empirical way of treating natural right, no *criterion* to determine whether one thing is fortuitous or necessary, whether it belongs to the state of nature or that of right. The maxim of preserving what man in actuality needs is *a posteriori*, [2] and is, hence, no *criterion*.

Moreover, the unification brought about by fear of the intolerableness of war, or motived by other particular aims, is accidental. It is the " empty name of a formless and external harmony," [3] inadequate to the notion of ethical organic totality. For the individual in such an inorganic union is not yet one with the whole. The natural and spiritual elements still gape asunder. They are the " split-up moments of the organic ethicality." [4] The absolute Idea of Ethicality contains the natural and spiritual as identical. The natural is not to be given up,

1. See Hegel's Werke, VII, p. 339.
2. *Ibid.*
3. *Ibid.*, p. 341.
4. *Ibid.*, p. 342.

while no abstracted side, natural as well as spiritual, may be exalted to generality.

However, the empirical standpoint has its advantage. It keeps in contact with actual life. Through the practical exercise of right the individual stands amidst the inter-connection of things, lives in the vital intuition (*Anschauung*) of the whole. In this respect the empiricists are right in preferring their inconsistency to the unpractical theory of the philosopher and metaphysician. Hegel admitted this point deliberately, for, according to his own view, the living exercise of right constitutes an essential ingredient of the State which he designates as the "absolute ethicality."

In the second part of the treatise Hegel proceeds to criticize the Kantian theory of natural right, to which that of Fichte is appended. The Kantian theory, like many others, starts with the individual as a social atom. The being of the individual is set out as the first and highest. This way of considering the problem Hegel called *anti-socialistic*.

However, in one important point, Kant and Fichte differ from the wrong kind of natural right theory which culminates in eudæmonism. That is the standpoint of infinity or unlimitedness (*Unendlichkeit*). To be determinate, they hold that the individual through his pure rationality is established on his own basis. He obeys no external law, but only the universally valid norm of practical reason.

That pure rationality, however, on account of the Kantian dualism, remains metaphysical. It turns against the world of experience. Here Hegel is at one with Schelling's Identity-Philosophy in holding that the antithesis between the manifoldness of natural events and the unity of ethical law must be overcome. The Idea must be the "indifference point" between the two opposites. Kant forbids all empirical consideration in ethical determination. The ethical will must be autonomous, i. e., free from the influence of motives and considerations derived from empirical grounds. Hegel, on the other hand, wants to exhibit the causal necessity of empirical events and the freedom of moral will as attributes of one substance. The ethical exists in the finite appearance as well as in the infinite reason.

According to Kant, the criterion of moral law consists not in the content, but in the form, of will; not in *what* is willed, but in *how* it is willed. In other words, it consists in the *willed* universal validity of the maxim, in the intention and disposition to abide by the law.

Such a moral law is, Hegel complains, empty. Out of it no concrete knowledge can be deduced, since it lacks all the substance of law and the material of will. It says nothing as to what in all circumstances is to be willed and done, except in the mere assertion of the pure form (A = A); but says all about what is not to be willed and not to be done (A is not Non-A). It is, therefore, negative and tautological. Hegel is of the opinion that it is indifferent to such formal moral law whether it be filled up with a certain material of right and duty at all. And it also lies beyond the capacity of the law-giving practical reason to decide whether this or an opposite concrete determination is to be recognized. To ask the pure practical reason the question, "What is right and duty?" is the same as to ask formal Logic, "What is true?" In both cases it is like milking a he-goat. [1]

Moreover, the tautological formula, when pushed to its logical consequence, simply results in the formal conversion of any arbitrary maxim into absolute law. [2] For the formalism which excludes every concrete determination would enable any abstract determination which constitutes the content of the maxim of a particular will, to be exalted to universality. [3] This proceeding of passing from the particular to the universal Hegel designates as the "principle of unethicality." Nay, he denounces it as "smuggling" and "jugglery." [4]

Fichte's endeavor, which in Hegel's view is the logical outcome of the Kantian theory, to secure the agreement of conduct with moral law through compulsion by government and that in turn through the superintendence of an "Ephorate," proves no more successful. For compulsion is external and contrary to the principle of freedom.

1. See Hegel's Werke, VII, p. 352.
2. *Ibid.*, pp. 352–356.
3. *Ibid.*, p. 354.
4. *Ibid.*, pp. 352–356.

Hegel's interest lies in the specification of the ethical life, by which it develops into a concrete system of moral laws. It will not do to posit a formal moral law on the one hand, a state of natural existence on the other. The antithesis between reason and nature, the universal and the particular, must be reconciled. So Hegel's philosophical mission consists in comprehending and exhibiting the ethicality in the social and historical life of men as a totality in unity with the Idea (The Universal or Absolute).

In the third part of the treatise Hegel offers as his own position the Philosophy of Ethicality. [1] It turns upon the complete totality of living national life. The spirit which manifests itself as objective spirit in the absolute ethicality of a whole nation is here conceived as the Absolute. [2] In the absolute ethical life the ideal or subjective moment of morality and the real or objective moment of the *ethos* are one. The dualism of Kant is overcome, but the difficulty centers around the problem of bringing the ethical spirit of the individual into unison with the absolute ethicality so that the former forms a pulse-beat [3] of the latter.

Absolute ethicality, Hegel insists, is the ethicality of all. It is the universal spirit pervading the whole nation. As the individual is a member, but not the ground of the whole, the ethical spirit of the individual must be dominated by the absolute ethicality. If the individual moral principle is exalted to be the supreme norm of objective, absolute ethicality, it means the "deepest despotism and total ruin of the Idea of ethical organization." [4] Or, what amounts to the same thing, if a part organizes itself and withdraws from the dominion of the whole, there disease sets in and the death of the whole begins. [5]

1. Hegel treated the same theme in the "System der Sittlichkeit," which is in substance identical with the sphere of "Objective Spirit" in the later form of his complete system.
2. It appears that Hegel at this time has not reached the "Absolute Spirit," but believes that the spheres of Art, Religion, and Pure Philosophy can be comprised in the "Objective Spirit," i.e., in the Absolute Ethicality.
3. Werke, VII, p. 392.
4. *Ibid.*, p. 406.
5. *Ibid.*, p. 404.

The element of the absolute ethicality in the individual shows itself in the adherence and devotion of the individual to the nation. This is seen in war, where the individual must sacrifice himself for the whole. A nation which can carry on war proves itself thereby to be ethically healthy. That is to say, it has some higher aspiration beyond natural existence, and its individuals are so earnest in standing for and upholding this ideal that they are willing to die for it. In this connection Hegel energetically rejects Kant's ideal of everlasting Peace.

In this view of ethicality as primarily the ethicality of a whole nation, Hegel has availed himself of the teachings of Aristotle and some others of the ancients. For them, too, the whole is more essential than the parts. The nation is prior to the individual. " The child must be nursed at the breast of universal ethical life." [1] " To live conformably to the *ethos* of one's country is to become ethical." [2] The best education for one's son is to " make him the citizen of a well-organized nation." [3] In short, for Hegel as for some Greek teachers, the ethical Idea attaches to the whole nation. The individuals must learn to live up to it through the discipline of ethically organized society. To reject the influence of the current of ethical society is as absurd as to try to avoid breathing or the circulation of blood.

From the viewpoint of the ethical Hegel works the spheres of economical, legal, and moral, all into one another. For him the physical needs of man and their satisfactions also enter, as an essential moment, into the totality of life. An ethical philosophy cannot be completed without having touched upon them. But to the system of absolute ethical life this economical moment with its inward nullity must be subordinated. The problem, therefore, for Hegel is to adjust the economical to the ethical. The first and rudimentary step is through the institution of *Right*.[4] Hence there arises a threefold organization: (1) the economical sphere, (2) the legal sphere, and (3) the ethical sphere. According to the notion of totality all the three

---

1. Werke, VII, p. 395.
2. *Ibid.*, p. 396.
3. Diog. Laert, VIII, sec. 16.
4. See below p. —— - note.

moments must be incorporated in the absolute ethical. But this proves not to be the case in reality. So Hegel here takes over from Plato the differentiation of social *Stände* in the State.

In analogy with Plato Hegel articulates the members of a nation into three *Stände:*

(1) The *Stand* of freemen, i. e., statesmen and soldiers;

(2) the *Stand* of the *bourgeois;*

(3) the *Stand* of the peasants.

The first *Stand* leads a completely universal life; the second has its sphere characterized by possession, property, and rights, while the third in its rudimentary work has to do only with the earth as element. Again, in the spirit of ancient thought, Hegel imposes upon the second and third *Stände* the task of relieving the first *Stand* from manual work and the cares of possession and property, so that its members may devote themselves exclusively to public life. But one more important point Hegel insists upon in organizing the individuals into distinct *Stände* is to make the content of ethical life spiritually so rich and variegated that it furnishes a favorable environment and abundant opportunity to produce genius, talent, and highly-gifted individuals. Such individuals [1] will, through their ingenious works in any sphere of Art and knowledge *(Wissenschaft)*, elevate and enliven the outlook of the ethical life. Hegel disparages [2] the Roman régime of a flat level of mere legal persons, where incentives to the development of extraordinary individuals are wanting.

In such an ethical organization the different individuals are according to their nature established in different stations to which are attached corresponding and appropriate duties. Hence, while volition and effort are necessary for moral activity, it is needless for them to reflect upon what to will and what to do or to consider whether the common aims propounded for daily accomplishment are also good and right.

But, according to Hegel, the absolute ethicality is embodied only in the first *Stand* — that of freemen. To the *bourgeois* is accorded a relative ethicality, whereas the peasants possess an unorganic ethicality

1. Werke, VII, pp. 385-387 ; cf. K. Fischer : *op. cit.*, pp. 287, 288.
2. Werke, VII, pp. 380-381.

only. In this respect Hegel is rather unjust. The ethical virtue of the *bourgeois* and peasants in working for the interest of the physical needs and satisfaction of the whole, in duty-fulfilling, in creating possession and property, and thereby bringing substantial strength to the nation, is not sufficiently appreciated. True, there is a difference of degree in the importance of services rendered by the several *Stände*. But so far as all perform an essential function, the ethical value of none can be denied. And it is logically inconsistent to insist first that the absolute ethicality is the all-pervading spirit *in* and *of* the whole nation, and then to locate its seat in the first *Stände* only.

Hegel was out of sympathy with vague cosmopolitanism, the empty "Rights of Man" and the idea of a world-republic. Influenced by the teaching of Montesquieu he adheres to the essentiality of national idiosyncrasy as conditioned through climate, age, etc. To Hegel, however, the definite form of the ethical life of a nation is not opposed to the univeresal reason, but united with and penetrated by it. Here Hegel takes over the "potency-theory" of Schelling which recurs in the *Phänomenologie* as the theory of stages. "The totality of life is in the nature of the polyp, just as in the nature of the nightingale and the lion. So the world-spirit has in every form its hollower or more developed, but absolute self-feeling, and in every nation, under every whole of *ethos* and laws, its being (*Wesen*), and enjoys its self." [1]

Again, in so far as every nation itself exhibits a spiritual whole, there are also stages in the life of the nation. Every stage of a nation just like every stage of the objective spirit exhibits a self-contained whole, which carries in itself an Absolute right. So feudalism and slavery, at times when the genius of a nation has not yet come to full unfolding, are for that stage the absolute truth.

The passage from one stage of Spirit to another takes place according to Hegel by fits and starts. The view of the gradual development in history under the influence of the stage-theory is deepened into a theory of periodical jerks. Here a deeper justification for revolution in states is germinally found. And the accusation against Hegel as standing for finalism is clearly unjust.

1. Werke, VII, p. 409.

CHAPTER II

THE SYSTEM OF ETHICALITY

This posthumous work was written immediately after the Treatise on Natural Right [1] had been finished. The treatise had set forth the Hegelian absolute ethicality in a sketchy way. Now this "System" undertakes to develop the same standpoint in a more comprehensive manner. In germ it contains all the three aspects of the later "Philosophy of Spirit." Discussions on both Subjective and Objective Spirit appear here inseparably side by side. Lines also point to the sphere of absolute spirit. But ostensibly all these spheres were for the time being held together through and in the notion of Ethicality.

Owing to Hegel's striving after systematic architectonic, his material, here as elsewhere, organizes itself into a triplicity. The first section of it deals with what may be called "natural ethicality." It expounds essentially the ethical consciousness of individual man, not the self-conscious *morale*, but the agitation through something foreign, i. e., Nature. This is followed by an antithesis (in the second section) which Hegel designates as the Negative or Freedom or *Verbrechen*. Freedom here means relief from natural ethicality — freedom to have its world in itself. It is the standpoint of radical subjectivism. To any universalist theorist of Ethics it is no wonder that such subjectivism appears as infringement or crime *(Verbrechen)*. The third section expounds the absolute ethicality. It is substantially a repetition in a different form of what has been offered in the Treatise on Natural Right. Unfortunately this section, as it stands, was not completed by the philosopher.

Hegel wants to get away from the one-sided subjective standpoint of the Kantian moral philosophy. This innovation he started in the Treatise on Natural Right and carried further in this "System of

1. For the sake of abbreviation this phrase will hereafter be employed to designate the essay concerning the Scientific Modes of Treating Natural Right.

14

Ethicality." For Kant the moral law is the fundamental law of a rational world which stands behind and over against the world of appearance. From Hegel's moral standpoint, however, the moral law is also actualized in the objective world. In other words, Hegel conceives Ethicality as the system of the living *ethos* of a nation. Hence, for him, Ethics expands into an exposition of the whole corporate life of a nation.

Life is a dynamical notion. It signifies a reciprocal action and reaction of subject and object. Nay, it signifies the totality as subject-object. The subjective aspect Hegel distinguishes and designates as notion or conception, the objective as intuition (*Anschauung*). The absolute ethicality is to be exhibited as the identity, i. e., the reciprocal implication, of both aspects

Hegel begins his exposition with the individual man. The unification of the universal and particular in the individual man he calls " Absolute Ethicality in the form of Relation." [1] The universal at first manifests itself in the individual in the form of impulse or instinct striving after satisfaction. It is an inner " tension " because of an inner " discord." The inner unity and peace can be restored only when satisfaction is attained. The ethical element here consists in the transcendence or resolution of the " discord." The particular is adjusted to the universal, or the intuition (*Anschauung*) is subsumed under the notion.

While the " discord " continues the individual man is in the state of need or want; when it is transcended he attains enjoyment. The transition from need to enjoyment is effected through Labor *(Arbeit)*. Labor serves to satisfy need and thereby to secure enjoyment. Both Labor and enjoyment involves subsumption of object under subject. But in the latter the subsumption is more complete. It becomes ideal. [2]

It is to be noticed that Hegel has here come to recognize the ethical value of labor, whereas in the Treatise on Natural Right he had done injustice to the claim of Labor. His comprehension of the significance of Labor has essentially deepened.

1. Hegel's Werke, VII, pp. 421 f.
2. *Ibid.*, p. 425.

The moments in Labor are occupancy, production and possession or preservation. The formation of Capital is here by Hegel supplied with moral justification. For Capital is conceived by our thinker as Labor saved up.

Labor differentiates itself into mechanical work, plantation, domestication of animals, and formation or cultivation of human beings. The last moment, which alone has ethical importance, is the acme of human labor. This again differentiates itself into sexual love, parental love, and education.[1]

In sexual love the relation between the loving parties persists in feeling which desires its object. But both the sides affected are on an equality to each other. "Each intuits or perceives itself in the other, while the other remains another. This unintelligibility of the being of oneself in another belongs to the natural moment, not to the ethical; for this is, in reference to the differentiated, the absolute identity of both."[2]

Sexual love is not the pure expression of love, since the impelling factor here is desire, i. e., something sensual. The purity of love is thereby disturbed. The ideal relation founded on love between man and woman is that between brother and sister as is manifested in the "Antigone."[3]

Upon sexual love follows the relation of parents to children. The problem here is the dominance of parents over children, the subsumption of object under subject. But in parental love there is no desire. It ends not in sensual feeling, as with sexual love, but in a complete independent individuality. In this complete independent individual "the parents perceive their unity as reality. They are it themselves, and it is their forth-born, visible identity and medium."[4]

---

1. A detailed discussion of these three moments of life here, under the head of Labor, appears to be out of its proper place, but the reason is perhaps that this posthumous work, just because it was not completed nor published, had not been well organized.
2. Hegel's Werke, VII, p. 429.
3. See below, pp. 30-32.
4. Hegel's Werke, VII, p. 431.

The highest step of Labor in the formation of human beings is the education of man. Education for Hegel is the elevation of particularity to universality. Here feeling, need, desire, all fall silent; and universal intelligence dominates the whole situation. With education the step of fullest universality is reached.

As has been pointed out, [1] from Hegel's moral standpoint Ethics expands into a systematic exposition of the whole corporate life of a nation. Now life is a manifold process. The individual needs many things for complete living. He can himself carry on only one or a few kinds of work, "the rest of what he needs is acquired in another way — through the labor of other men." [2] Hence a division of labor among many intelligent individuals is a natural course.

Division of labor leads to skill, facility, and improvement and, consequently, a surplus of production over the totality of needs. Such a surplus loses its direct interest for the subject. " As there is, in regard to the subject, an abstraction of need in general, so surplus (on the other hand) furnished a general possibility of use." [3]

Surplus gives rise to possession. Possession becomes property when it is legitimated through legal right. Thus in property " the thoroughgoing ideality and the true potency of practical intelligence " [4] actually begin. For Right is the first step in objective spirit. Through the legitimation of Right, the system of physical needs is elevated into the realm of ideality.

The passage of possession or property from one subject to another is first through barter, subsequently by contract. But in contract the passage has been transformed from a real one to an ideal. The ideal, however, is binding, is the truly necessary. To secure this, there must be some universal " binding medium " which assures the performance of the contract. As such a medium nothing can serve but an objective ideal inter-connection (*Zusammenhang*)—what Hegel designates "Spirit." [5]

1. See before, p. 15.
2. Hegel's Werke, VII, p. 437.
3. *Ibid.*, p. 438.
4. *Ibid.*, p. 443.
5. *Ibid.*

It is what Aristotle calls " active reason," and the Stoics the universal World-Reason.

The above-mentioned Spirit or Reason is in the strict sense the essential part of Man. Owing to its universal presence in all human beings Equality has been made the guiding principle in the realm of Right. But human life is not so simple and abstract; hence the principle of Equality does not always apply. The difficulty is that in the actual relations of life the " living individuals stand towards one another with unequal power of living." [1] So the relation turns out to be one of ruler and subject or master and slave. [2] The subsumption here is, therefore, only external.

There is, however, one natural relation in which the identity of the antithesis appears not as subjugation of one to another but throughout as an ethical inner identity. This is the institution of the Family.

The Family is the last link in natural ethicality. Within the family the categories of private property, contract, and legal right have no place. "The work is distributed according to the nature of each member, but the product is common to all." [3] So the whole family has only one common property. " The husband is the master and administrator but not the proprietor in contrast with the other members of the family." [4] And " as administrator he has only the appearance of free disposition." [5]

The origination of this relation begins with marriage. Marriage, Hegel repeatedly insists, never was a contract. For contract can be made concerning appropriable things only, not free individuals. And contract can be annulled at will, whereas marriage is a spiritual permanent bond.

This peculiarity is enhanced by the advent of the child. The child is that member of the family which comes to elevate the contract-

1. Hegel's Werke, VII, p. 445.
2. *Ibid.*, p. 446.
3. *Ibid.*, p. 448.
4. *Ibid.*
5. *Ibid.*

like union. It is " the *raison d'être* of the relation." [1] Herewith natural ethicality reached its climax.

The second section of the " System of Ethicality " treats of the antithesis or the contra-ethical. It is, as has been mentioned in the second paragraph of the present chapter, designated by Hegel as the Negative, or Freedom, or Infringement. The execution here is much more sketchy and synoptic than in the other sections. In the later " Encyclopædia of Philosophical Sciences " and " The Philosophy of Right " Hegel has at the corresponding place let " Subjective Morality " come to its due. For, to him who takes Ethics to be through and through objective, moralistic subjectivism stands just on the same footing as Crime or Infringement.

In the first section the Universal has been considered as lodged in the particularity, i. e., the Ethical as conditioned by motives of natural need; and it stayed mainly with the realm of Right. Now, in the second section, the point is that the individual strives to come forward as Universality, that is, subjectivity seeks to set up itself as the Absolute. The process is one of liberation from the realm of natural ethicality and a pressing on to the Absolute. But the step is taken in such a violent way that it leads to a sheer breach or infringement and Life itself is thereby injured.

The Negative or the Pure Freedom in this way pushes on to an annihilation of the objective, and hence to a plain destruction of life. Such Negation must be re-negated or counteracted. This is done through punishment or " retributive justice." [2]

Punishment or retributive justice is the moral balance due to the trespasser *(Verbrecher)*. It is virtually demanded by him. For only thereby can his wrong be undone, and his personal integrity reëstablished. If he takes the proper attitude of a rational being towards his own act, as Socrates did, he will receive it gratefully.

---

1. Hegel's Werke, VII, p. 449.
2. *Ibid*, p. 453, also cf. below, pp.———.

Punishment, however, is only the real counteraction wrought
through an external law court. It is not the ideal counteraction render-
able in the inner court of Conscience. Such ideal counteraction is found
only in the "guilty conscience *(böses Gewissen)*"[1] of the offender.
Guilty conscience occurs at the moment when the offender comes to
realize that he has injured the Idea of Life. He thought to destroy
something alien, but unhappily wronged Life itself. Now he comes to
experience in conscience the reaction of what is injured and feel his own
nullity or worthlessness. This is an inner spiritual conversion of the
subjectivity formerly disposed to deny anything objective.

Now Hegel goes on to examine the whole list of crimes or infringe-
ments. Physical destruction, robbery, theft, murder, revenge, the duel,
etc., all are discussed at length. His treatment in this part, however,
seldom attains the height of philosophical discourse. It is plain, sober
and commonplace, and lacking in ethical import.

In the third section we expect a full exposition of the absolute
ethicality. But, as has been pointed out at the beginning of the present
chapter, what we find is in the main only a repetition of what has been
offered in the Treatise on Natural Right and unfortunately was not
completed by our philosopher. It nevertheless reveals for the first time
in the "System of Ethicality" the true harmony of the individual with
the universal Spirit.

In the natural ethicality the Ethical was not present in the pure
form of Spirit. "There is an intransmutability of the element of nature
in it."[2] In the infringing subjectivity the ethical comes to the stage
only in a negative way as a counter-action. The absolute ethical,
however, must step forth in the positive form of Spirit. This happens in
an ethical nation.

The nation, or rather the ethical nation, is "the *Anschauung* of the
Idea of Ethicality, the form in which the Idea appears from the side of its
particularity."[3] In an ethical nation the individual perceives every

1. Hegel's Werke, VII, p. 453.
2. *Ibid.*, p. 464.
3. *Ibid.*, p. 466.

other individual as himself, because of the "identity of intelligence" which is the essence of ethical life. "According to nature the man sees flesh of his flesh in the woman; but according to ethicality he sees spirit of his spirit." [1]

It is, however, not the individual which affirms itself in the Ethical, but the universal absolute Spirit. "In ethicality, therefore, the individual is in an universal mood; his empirical being and doing are a *plain universal;* for it is not the individual who behaves, but the universal Absolute Spirit in him." [2]

There is, however, a difference of degree in the adequacy and extent to which the individual represents the universal, or the latter manifests itself in him. And, conformably, the value of the individuals varies.

Here follows the discussion on State-constitution and government. The reason for interweaving politics with Ethics [3] is that if the Ethical is lodged in the objective, in the transcendedness of the singular individual, further determinate relations must, for the sake of the actualization of the Ethical, be established among the many individuals. Hence comes politics. Ethics, however, is the foundation of politics. The political organization of the whole nation is an expression of the ethical Idea. And the articulation of the individuals into several *Stände* is based upon the differences of level among their ethical aims.

The ethicality in the individual is virtue. The "Absolute ethicality," however, is "the indifference of all virtues." It appears not as *love to* fatherland and nation and law, but as the absolute *life in* the fatherland and *for* the nation." [4] So bravery or valor appears as the highest virtue. It consists in the complete uplifting or elevation of the individual to the universal.

The relatedness of the Ethical to the national State has, with Hegel, its basis in the paramount necessity of the rôle which a national culture fostered by State organization plays in the actualization of the ethical

---

1. Hegel's Werke, VII, p. 465.
2. *Ibid.*
3. Cf. above, pp. 1, 2, and below, pp. ———.
4. Hegel's Werke, VII, p. 469.

Idea. But owing to this stringent association of national State and Ethicality, Hegel stamps on his universalism a mark of national individualism. For he will not let Humanity (or Mankind) organize itself into an Ethical whole. International relations are not brought under ethical valuation. [1]

The form of " relative ethicality " creates Right and is righteousness. [2] Here as in the Treatise on Natural Right Hegel will not allow as much significance to the administration of justice as Kant did. For right is relative to possession and property, which appear to the advocate of the universal as " *bourgeois*." For Hegel the *Bürger* has no proper sense for the absolute Ethicality. As we have said in dealing with the Treatise on Natural Right, Hegel, having adopted a universalist way of thinking and entertained the Platonic ideal of the State, naturally speaks of the *bourgeois* spirit and the standpoint of Right contemptuously. But it should not be forgotten that Hegel saw in Right the reflection of the ideality and regarded it as the first step of Objective Spirit. So he connects Right organically with Ethicality, and does not oppose the one to the other as Kant does.

Finally the " elementary ethicality " is the spirit of "trust " of the peasants' *Stand*. " It is not through understanding . . . that it is to be set in motion, but through the wholeness of trust and adaptation to the demand of the situation, through external impelling to the whole." [3]

The moments of ethicality appear respectively in the forms of the three *Stände*. The "freemen " fulfill the absolute ethical aims. The *bourgeois* contribute taxes and gifts. The peasants provide for physical needs. But the complete vitality of the three ethical " potencies " manifests itself only in their organized totality, not in any single *Stand* as Hegel's occasional unguarded expressions might imply. [4]

One more point to be noticed here is that in the Treatise on Natural Right Hegel allows the peasants' *Stand* only an unorganic morality because their work has to do only with nature or the soil as the element.

1. See below, p. ———.
2. Hegel's Werke, VII, p. 472.
3. *Ibid.*, p. 473.
4. Cf. above, p. 12.

Now he sees that while the *bourgeois* incline towards private ends, the peasants have their work and earning directed towards greater and more comprehensive totality, and are capable of a courage which belongs to absolute ethicality. So he turns more in favor of the peasants' *Stand* than the *bourgeois*.

Now our philosopher proceeds to consider the problem of government, through which the ethical system is exhibited. Hegel regards government as above the three *Stände*, and so places it in the hands of priests and the elders. These officials are recruited from the first *Stand*, the *Stand* of freemen. But as soon as they ascend to the last status they live absolutely in the ideal moments.

The relation of government to the *Volk* is conceived by Hegel as that of organism to the inorganic, that of spirit to physique. The government is nothing particular or finite, it is " the absolute power," " the appearance of God." [1] Further theocratic expressions are employed, but they seldom throw much light on the real issue.

In order to carry out its aims, the government must have central power. Here Hegel divides government into absolute government and general government. The former comprehends what is designated as the princely and lawgiving power, the latter what is called the adminstrative power, in the later " Philosophy of Rights." But Hegel does not allow any sharp " separation of powers," for the unitary character of the government must be strictly preserved.

As moments of the general government recur the systems of needs, of justice, and of discipline. Besides what has in other connections been said of these moments, Hegel advocates here a State regulation of economic affairs, while natural adjustment is still allowed a wide room to play. State law may check the natural tendency to great inequality of wealth and the consequent formation of a few enormous private fortunes. Such enormous private fortunes simply become brute might, and induce their possessors to withdraw from the organic whole and to disdain anything high and noble. When such a state of things comes into existence the ethical disappears.

1. Hegel's Werke, VII, p. 487.

The discussion on administration of justice and discipline or education here does not offer us anything strikingly original, except that Hegel
charges the State with a higher task than mere administration of justice,
that is, with the fostering of culture.   The work thus finds its end
without completion.

CHAPTER III

THE PHENOMENOLOGY OF SPIRIT

This work of Hegel appeared in 1807. It is the first great work written and published by the philosopher. As the author describes it as his " voyage of discovery," so the phases of experience it describes are extraordinarily fresh and illuminating.

To begin with a few remarks in the way of general characterization, the " Phenomenology of Spirit " is the categorical development and unfolding of the forms of Spirit, while the whole variegated actual life is a succession of the ever self-developing moments of the same. The manifold moments of actual life form a system which in a certain way closely corresponds [1] to that of the dialectic unrolling of logical forms The reason for such correspondence is simply that they are both only the different aspects of one and the same Absolute Spirit. The historical actuality, therefore, is the categorical steps of consciousness objectified, and the development of the latter is an abbreviation of the unfolding stages of Absolute Spirit.

The Absolute Spirit gives itself at every determinate time, in every determinate nation, a determinate form. Each of these forms has its relative justification, but none of them holds good for all times and all nations. They do not, however, stand separately one beside another, but reveal in the more interlaced life a higher development of Spirit.

As has been hinted [2] Hegel started with the aim of overcoming the Kantian subjectivism. The Reason, he insists, must be objectified. The first step for such objectification was made by Schelling, in his conceiving nature as a rational whole. But the metaphysical fundamental event *(Erlebnis)* for Schelling is Nature, whereas for Hegel it is the historico-social life of mankind. Thus Hegel transcended the Identity-philosophy through the notion of Spirit.

1. See below, pp. ———.
2. See before, pp. 8–10 and 14–15.

25

Spirit is conceived by Hegel as life and actuality, and the essence of it is development. Now the "Phenomenology of Spirit" offers to unfold and unroll the steps of the development of Spirit. It interweaves the subjective and objective moments closely together and points out the way of its liberation and elevation from the lowest level of sensuous certainty to the highest of Absolute Knowledge.

For the purpose of a study of Hegel's ethical teaching the part on "Spirit" is by far the most important portion and demands careful consideration. But, in the preceding parts also, discussions with direct ethical bearings are to be found.

In the part on "Self-consciousness" Hegel describes the nature of Man as desire and will to might, or as striving to subjugate nature and make it his own. A limit to this striving is found when another self-consciousness comes into play. And, on the other hand, a self-consciousness cannot attain its satisfaction apart from other self-consciousness. Hence, common life through mutual recognition is an inevitable course.

This mutual recognition is the result of a development from the lowest grades of group-life such as are manifested in the relations of master and slave, etc., up to the form of Spirit. It finds full expression in Right, which is the first stage or grade within objective Spirit. In dealing with the institution of slavery the value and significance of labor is fully discussed by Hegel.

The life of slavery is mainly a physical existence. The extreme antithesis to it is Stoicism which pretends to be entirely independent of the physical. This is absolutely one-sided and for that reason untenable. Then comes the anarchy and chaos of Skepticism and the "unhappy consciousness" of Medieval dualism. Especially in regard to dualism, Hegel urges that the illusive idea of a Beyond, nay, an opposite absolute, must be done away with. Here, in this world, lies the abode and path of Eternal Spirit. Our secular life must not be considered as worthless as Medieval Christianity held it to be. The unity of this world and its opposite must be restored. This is achieved through the effect of the all-permeating and all-embracing " Reason."

Reason, however, once enthroned in the world, requires a radical reorganization of the ideal of life. That is, it starts within the sphere of social philosophy a Dialectic, which must be carried to further and further development. Thus the natural unconscious ethical unity inwardly decomposes itself and leads through the moment of consciousness to a higher synthesis where harmony is reinstated in a new form.

In the "Phenomenology" Hegel verifies the whole process by an appeal to abundant historical facts, while not expressly referring to them. Here, as in the "System of Ethics," he begins the series of the stages of the "Actualization of Rational Self-consciousness through itself," with a short description of Greek life as absolute ethicality. The individual and society there naturally and unconsciously form a perfect unity. The individual consciousness does not stand over against the universal. His action and existence are not distinct from the general ethical substance. The " I " is the " we " and the " we " is the " I." There is harmony without discord.

It is true that the ethical spirit in Greek life is identical with the *ethos*. That is, it is still substance, not yet subject. However, " the individual recognizes the *ethos* not only as what constitutes his universal objective nature as a thing, but apprehends or beholds himself in it, or recognizes it as particularized in his own individuality and that of his fellow members." [1] Therefore, when the ethicality agrees with the *ethos* it embraces the total life of a nation. Hence, the individual spirit is also the universal.

However, this beautiful Paradise of mankind must come to an end. The natural (*naturhaft*) ethical existence of the Greeks cannot display the maximum of the value of life. It must, by its inner dialectical necessity, be led through the Purgatory of Reason. The rigid or conventional trust of the individual in the universal bond, i.e., in the *ethos* and law of the nation, cannot endure. Ethicality becomes intelligible and intelligent. This inaugurates the age of moral individualism and subjectivism.

---

1. Hegel's Werke: " Phänomenologie des Geistes," herausgegeben von G. Lasson, p. 233, Baillie's Translation, p. 343.

Sophistry, Stoicism, the Natural Right of the Renaissance and Kantian moral Subjectivism are several forms of this type of consciousness.

One general feature observable in the above-named forms of consciousness is that, to quote Hegel, "Self-consciousness enters upon its path or pilgrimage with the determination to be, as individual spirit, itself the essential reality." [1] Or what comes to the same thing, " it plunges into life and brings the pure individuality to fruition or accomplishment." [2] It recognizes no bondage, only the " I " and its desire. Again it wants to traverse, in its elevated self-feeling, the world in itself. " It does not so much make its own happiness as grasp it directly and enjoy it." [3]

In enjoyment, however, the individual finds the germ of self-destruction. For the natural world may not comply with his desire or wish. Hence he passes over to action and deed, i.e., to the betterment of the world. In other words the "law of the heart " [4] is the individuality taken for the universal, the universal to be actualized. The world, therefore, is to be made subject to this law.

However, thanks to the latent but perpetual working of Dialectic, the individual must come to see that the true good lies in the self-sacrifice of mere individuality. And he also must pass through the experience of learning that the course of the world is not so evil as it appears to him. The individual, therefore, has to give up his heaven-storming, world-bettering, and world-blessing tendency and pass over into the pleased and pleasing play of powers among the individuals themselves.

Furthermore, the rationally self-conscious individual has to make the experience that there is still something which rises high above the subjectivism of the individual. That is the " Spiritual essence " which " is the essence of all essence." [5] Therewith we have, through a

---

1. Hegel's Phän., p. 236, Baillie's Trans., p. 347.
2. *Ibid.*, p. 238., *B. T.*, p. 351.
3. *Ibid.*
4. *Ibid.*, p. 241, *B. T.*, p. 357.
5 *Ibid.*, p. 273, *B. T.*, p. 408.

spiral development of the phenomenology of consciousness, reached the standpoint which Hegel designates as " Spirit " in the closer sense of the term which is, as we have hinted before, [1] the chief matter of ethical concern in the " *Phenomenology of Spirit*."   Now we leave the sphere of subjective spirit and set foot on the field of Objective Spirit, of an all-embracing, universally valid inter-connection of life.

A.   *True Spirit: Ethicality*

The steps of " True Spirit " or Objective Spirit differentiate themselves from those of subjective individual spirit through the fact that they are not mere forms of consciousness, but are " the ethical life of a nation," i. e., real actualities, or " forms of a world." [2]   As the two moments of the " Spirit " which governs the ethical world, Hegel set up two laws, the law of common stock and that of common life-order.   The one, having its root in the depth of the make-up of the nation, is called subterranean law, or divine law, since it is of immemorial origin, rules independently of human caprice and possesses universal validity; the other, comprehending within it known laws and morals, is human law; it arises out of common consciousness and is publicly proclaimed.   To the subterranean and divine law corresponds family piety, the elementary foundation of all ethicality and common life, whereas to human law corresponds civic life in the State.   The family is related to the State as the Penates are to the universal Spirit.

In the family the divine law prevails.   The relations of the members of the family to one another are those: (1) between husband and wife, (2) between parents and children, (3) between brothers and sisters.   The relation between husband and wife is characterized by the mutual recognition of equality, but is conditioned naturally, nay, even sexually, and rests on desire and pleasure.   Hence their love cannot be spoken of as the highest grade of love.   The relation between parents and children is characterized by the inequality of

1. See before, p. 26.
2. Hegel's Phän., p. 286, Baillie's Trans., pp. 433 – 44.

age, and is affected by deep emotion. Therefore the love between parents and children is not unmixed either. The relation between brothers or between sisters is disturbed by jealous feeling. Only between brother and sister the pure relation is found. It signifies the acme of love. For there exists the pure and unmixed relation of free human individuals without the fetter of sensuality. They are of the same blood which in them, however, has come to rest and equilibrium. They do not crave for one another nor surrender themselves one to the other, nor receive a self from the other.

The individual has one value as a member of the family and another as a citizen. As a member of the family in the realm of the Penates, his value lies in his birth to the very family, in his inborn individuality. As he was *such a* member of the family only once and comes never again as the same member, his significance here is unique and irrecoverable when once lost.

The value of the same individual as citizen, in the realm of public spirit, is quite different. It depends upon the way of his conduct and the general significance of the same. It is, in other words, estimated according to the service performed. There is nothing which is irrecoverable.

Therefore the support and cultivation of the individual as such is the business of the family and family piety. This cannot tolerate that the member after death be thrown away and exposed to wild animals or to the destructive forces of Nature. The guardian of this family piety, however, is the woman. This is seen in the classical tragedy of the "Antigone" of Sophocles. When the brother has fallen in war against the State and been condemned to the last dishonor and been thrown to wild animals for food, the sister, who feels herself as such and according to her nature, does not hesitate a moment to fulfill her sacred duty by burying the dead brother. "Thus the feminine as sister has the highest presentiment of ethical life," [1] and can bring natural ethicality to full expression.

1. Hegel's Phän., p. 296, Baillie's Trans., p. 451.

The brother, however, forms the binding link between the divine and human. In Hegel's own words, "He passes from the divine law under which he lived, over to the human."[1] That is, the man passes forth into the life of external actuality, and shapes there, in a conscious way, his destiny. This manly principle of deed, action, individual creation, however, must be supplemented by the womanly principle of implicit inner feeling, wherein it finds warmth and satisfaction. "In this way both sexes overcome the limitations of their natural being, and rise to their ethical significance. As distinct they divide among themselves the differentiæ which the ethical substance gives itself."[2]

In the section on Ethical Conduct Hegel ranks the family spirit as the unconscious spirit. The ethical consciousness in this stage is essentially "character" or disposition. That is, it grows up in a plant-like way from the existential underworld of the naturalistic spiritual essence. Through action, however, this simple, nay, even naïve ethical spirit, is highly horrified at the light of the day. For action always in one degree or another falls short of the purity and wholeness of Ethical spirit. "Only inaction, therefore, is innocent,"[3] while action is so essential that it serves to "bring forth what in the first instance lay shut up as a mere possibility and thereby to connect the unconscious with the conscious, the non-existent with the existent."

From action naturally arise faults. Now from fault just as naturally follows the destiny of the agent. In other words the agent must suffer the consequence of his action in order to know his fault. "Because we suffer we recognize that we are guilty."[5] Antigone suffered because she violated the state-law in devoting herself exclusively to the feeling of family piety.

1. Hegel's Phän., p. 297, Baillie's Trans., p. 453.
2. *Ibid.*
3. *Ibid.*, p. 304, *B. T.*, p. 465.
4. *Ibid.*, p. 305, *B. T.*, p. 467.
5. Sophocles' Antigone, 926, cited in Phän., p. 306, Baillie's Trans., 468.

The recognition of the above truth, however, amounts to an end of unconscious natural ethicality. "Therewith the agent gives up his 'character' and the reality of his self."[1] "The youth" thus "marches or steps out of the unconscious mode of existence, out of family-life and attains the individuality of community."[2]

The State-law and family piety appear in a certain measure as the two poles of common life. The "*Antigone*" expresses the conflict of these two principles, the great tragedy of human life or the radical cleavage in the nature of man. The final victory is of course with the State.

The highest duty of the State is to maintain the whole at the expense of individuals, to secure the supremacy of the commonweal over individual interests. Therefore, wherever the latter begin to isolate themselves from the ethical interest, to usurp the commonweal and endanger the whole, the State has to take measures, even so drastic a one as War, to prevent such development. It is unfortunate to have the tranquillity of the State at stake, but still worse it is to let the ethical interest take root in particularity and get stiff and paralyzed, and hence the whole fall to pieces and the spirit flee away. War can shake the stagnation and inertia of the ethical interest. It is, therefore, the best means to renew the health of the nation and rejuvenate the common existence.

State law is certainly superior to family piety. But the State should not be proud of its victory and abuse its supremacy. To quote Hegel's own words : "Public spirit has the root of its strength only in the underworld. The certainty felt by a nation, a certainty of which it is sure and which makes itself assured, finds the truth of its oath binding all its members into one, solely in the mute unconscious substance of all, in the waters of oblivion."[3] A State which builds itself up without having appropriated the fruitful and vitalizing value of the natural society, i. e., the family, does not build on

1. Hegel's Phän., p. 306, Baillie's Trans., 468.
2. *Ibid.*, p. 307, *B. T.*, p. 470.
3. *Ibid.*, pp. 308, 389, *B. T.*. p. 472.

solid ground. A social system should not be constructed through and through rationalistically, but should in an organic teleological way grasp the State as a natural *Zusammenhang*, whose valuable roots must reach out into the realm of the unconscious, otherwise it would dry up and become desolate. "Thus the consummation of the public spirit turns round into the opposite, and it learns that its . . . victory is rather its defeat." [1]

The community of ethical life sinks back into a régime of legal persons. Hegel views this transition as a lamentable declension. For he sees in Right only a poor residue of the ethical. And the split of the organic harmonious unity into mechanical, unconnected atoms means to him an ethical bankruptcy.

B. *Spirit in Self-Estrangement: The Discipline of Culture and Civilization*

In the second division of the part on " Spirit " Hegel traces the forms of the individual's struggle for a substantial spiritual life, i. e., the realm of civilization, the world of belief, enlightenment, absolute freedom, and the reign of terror. The world of culture and civilization is a kind of world which the spirit creates out of itself, but wherein it does not feel at home, but rather a stranger. This is the world of the Spirit in " self-estrangement." The objective embodiment of the spiritual life of the individual in political, economical, and other social institutions, is actually his own self, but seems altogether outside him. He seems estranged from his true self, and the estrangement seems his own doing. This spells a contradiction within self-consciousness. This contradiction can only be " removed by effort and struggle, for the individual spirit has to create or recreate for itself and by its own activity a universal objective spiritual realm, which it implies and in which alone it can be free and feel itself at home." [2]

Thus to the world of culture and civilization the spirit opposes a world of pure consciousness. Pure consciousness in the form of

1. Hegel's Phän., p. 309, Baillie's Trans., p. 472.
2. J. B. Baillie: Note in Hegel's Phenom. of Mind, pp. 486, 487.

religious certainty preserves the belief in the true and the good and perceives its fulfillment and completion in a world of belief where God rules, namely, in the community permeated by divine spirit and filled with devotion and gratitude, with the true spirit of service and praise.

"However, when the believing consciousness has attained the idea of God as spirit, religious devotion cannot remain as the state of meditating on God and sinking believingly into this idea (*Vorstellung*), but it must proceed to the point that God is really *thought*, and out of belief a pure insight must come forth as its consequence and fruit."[1] Hence the pure consciousness comprehends in itself both "Belief and Pure Insight." It is belief because it is a flight out of the actual world into the world beyond. It is thinking and insight, because it is the consciousness of essence, of the simple inner being.

Insight is indeed the consequence and fruit of belief, but as insight it must needs step forth against the state of believing consciousness and conceive it as its counterpart, as false insight, as error, as prejudice, i.e., as superstition, and fight against it as such. In this mode pure insight becomes Enlightenment.

The weakness of Enlightenment as against religious belief is that it does not know to penetrate into the depth of religious consciousness and so criticize it from within, but simply attacks it from without and, for that reason, in its judgement and contempt it misses the point. But when the religious consciousness sets out to defend itself and prove its foundation, it is already infected and gradually becomes enlightened belief.

The guiding concept for both enlightenment and enlightened belief is utility, i. e., the reference of all things sacred and secular alike to human well-being, and thereby to human will. Human will thus becomes unrestrained, and when it is exalted to the throne of the world, i. e., declared to be sovereign, it inaugurates the reign of Absolute Freedom.

1. K. Fischer, *op. cit.*, p. 391.

Absolute Freedom is antithetic to civilization. It holds that men are by nature equal. All the differences and inequalities in possessions and rank under the rule of culture and civilization are due to corrupted and corrupting political and economic arrangements. They must be rooted out. Absolute Freedom consists in levelling, in extermination of difference, in a real revolution of actuality. " In this Absolute Freedom, therefore, all social estates into which the whole has differentiated itself are suppressed." And all restriction on the individual consciousness is done away with. " His purpose becomes the universal purpose, his language the universal law, his work the universal achievement." " The individual consciousness is conscious of itself as immediately the universal will." [1]

But, as a matter of fact, the law never was made directly by all the individuals, but only through their representatives. And it is impossible that everybody should govern, but only a few in power. Now the few in power are guilty, because they violate the principle of universal equality (or flat level). The governed mass, too, are guilty, because they stand suspect of disloyalty. Either party regards the other as guilty, and as, for that reason, to be extinguished. Thus comes the reign of terror.

The fundamental dogma of Absolute Freedom that men are by nature equal cannot be vindicated. Rather the truth is that they are by nature unequal, but that equality of personality can be reached through the way of civilization and ethical arrangement for mutual recognition and moral worth. The undertaking of equalization or levelling necessitates cutting off heads, for they save inequalities of talent, knowledge, sentiment, etc. The French revolution expected that the terror of death would frighten away inequalities of mind up to the last trace. But " what is negated is the unachieved, unfulfilled monadic entity of Absolute Free Self." [2] " The absolute freedom and universal will no longer coincide with the individual self and its immediate actuality. This is to be considered as transcended, while absolute freedom subsists. It subsists, however, no longer as the unrefined will of all individuals,

1. Hegel's Phän., pp. 380, 381, Baillie's Trans., pp. 595, 596.
2. Ibid., 383, B. T., p. 599.

but as the unselfish or pure will and its pure self-consciousness." [1]   In other words " the new form of moral spirit has arisen." [2]

C. Spirit Certain of Itself: Morality

In the third and last division of the part on " Spirit " Hegel treated fully of this new form of moral spirit. It is Spirit certain of itself. Historically it found its development in the Kantian moral philosophy. [3]

The moral spirit here posits a circle of postulates and moves itself therein. This position Hegel calls the Moral View of the World or Moral Teleology. In these postulates " a whole nest of the most thoughtless contradictions " [4] is involved. This Hegel calls Dissemblance. Finally in the form of Conscience, the moral spirit comes to its self-certainty.

The issue before the Moral View of the World or Moral Teleology is the relation between morality and the world. Since moral purposes hold good unconditionally and are to be carried out, it is postulated that between morality and the world there exists no antithesis, but agreement and harmony. This is the first postulate or rather the general theme of all postulates in which the Moral Teleology or the Moral View of the World consists. To this first postulate also belongs the harmony of morality and happiness.

The natural world, however, is not merely the completely detached external medium in which the moral consciousness has to realize its purpose but is contained in the moral consciousness itself as its own nature, i. e., as the sensuous element in the form of impulse and inclination. [5] Hence, the second postulate, the harmony between morality and sensuousness. Without the validity of the first postulate the universe disparts itself into two opposite worlds of moral law and natural law. Without the validity of the second human nature disparts itself into two opposite spheres of duty and instinct, inclination, and impulse. The

1. K. Fischer, *op. cit.*, p. 403.
2. Hegel's Phän., p. 387, Baillie's Trans., p. 605.
3. Cf. K. Fischer, *op. cit.*, pp. 403 f.
4. Hegel's Phän., p. 404.
5. See Hegel's Phän., pp. 391, 392, Baillie's Trans., pp. 613, 614.

unity of the world-order requires the validity of the one, the unity of the moral self-consciousness requires the validity of the other.

The moral self-consciousness knows only one motive, pure duty. But in reference to nature and the world, duties and moral laws multiply themselves. This plurality of moral relations presupposes and demands a consciousness other than the human for their ground and sanction. Hence the third postulate of " a master and ruler of the world who brings about the harmony of morality and happiness and at the same time sanctifies duties in their multiplicity." [1]

In comparison with the divine consciousness, human consciousness, through its limitedness, appears so incomplete and through its sensuously-affected volition so impure, that happiness cannot be expected as something earned through merit, but only as something granted out of free grace. But the divine consciousness, nevertheless, distributes happiness according to merit, i. e., according to the service rendered.

Here, however, contradictions immediately arise, and the moral consciousness has arrived at a state of " Dissemblance." In the first place morality, according to the " Moral View of the World," must be complete, or it is not at all. It refuses to be disintegrated. Hereby, however, the second postulate, the harmony of morality and sensuousness, is shaken. For "this harmony or unity is only a postulated being. What is actually there is consciousness, or the opposition of sensuousness and pure consciousness." "Consciousness has, therefore, of itself to bring about an harmonious unity and to be constantly making progress in morality. The completion of this result, however, is deferred to the remote infinite." For " morality is only moral consciousness *qua* negative force," in making the sensuous element conformable to morality. " If the harmonious unity actually entered the life of consciousness as an actual fact, the moral consciousness would be done away with." " Morality *qua* consciousness, i. e., its actuality, passes away with the attainment of harmony; just as in the moral consciousness or actuality its harmony is not present." [2]

---

1. Hegel's Phän., p. 395, Baillie's Trans., p. 618.
2. *Ibid.*, pp. 392, 393, *B. T.*, pp. 615, 616.

" The completion is, therefore, not to be reached as an actual fact, it is to be thought of merely as an absolute task or problem, i.e., one which remains a problem pure and simple." [1] For it is absurd to " speak of a morality which is not consciousness, i.e., which is no longer actual. On the other hand " its content has nevertheless to be thought of as something which unquestionably ought to be and cannot remain a problem, no matter whether we imagine the moral consciousness as quite canceled in the attainment of this goal or not." [2] For otherwise there can be no complete morality and, therefore, according to the " Moral View of the World " no morality at all.

The result is, therefore, that moral life proves " an undertaking which at once ought to remain an undertaking and yet ought to be carried out." [3] Now the moral consciousness cannot possibly be in earnest with such a dilemmatic undertaking. So it must quit this position.

Again, in the individual and through individual acts, innumerable good things have been brought about in the world. But the moral consciousness appreciates individual acts but meagerly. It looks forward to the Absolute Good as the final end of the world. This Absolute Good is exalted far above all particular goods, but is unfortunately deferred to a future world as in a nebulous distance, where nothing can any longer be exactly discerned. So the net result is that the morality which exists in a middle state, i. e., in an incomplete stage, is as good as nothing at all. And, on the other hand, the absolute good is to be, but is not yet, carried out, and therefore nothing good is done.

Still more ridiculous and disquieting is it to think that, supposing we admit both the relative value of the morality of the middle state and the actuality of a constant progress from the middle state to the absolute goal, then the relative value of progressive morality is approaching more and more to its ruin, and, therefore, is a constant

1. Hegel's Phän., p. 393, Baillie's Trans., p. 615.
2. *Ibid*, Baillie's Trans., pp. 615, 616.
3. *Ibid.*, Baillie's Trans., p. 616.

sinking and perishing, seeing that by the attainment of the Absolute goal morality *qua* consciousness, *qua* negative force, i. e., its actuality, exists no longer.

Furthermore, " happiness as the reward of merit belongs to the farthest goal of time. And yet every present act should be good and pure. And every good act is a source of satisfaction and fortune. So what should not be in the present is made present *(zur Gegenwart)*. Consciousness, therefore, pronounces, through the deed, that it is not in earnest with the postulate." [1]

One more point still. If all middle-state morality is incomplete and, therefore, as good as not at all, and if yet happiness can be received out of free grace, and the divine consciousness distributes it, none the less according to relative merit, then the innermost sub-conscious motive of good conduct is happiness rather than morality, for there is no hope of accomplishing complete morality in the present state, while happiness may be hoped and expected.

Accordingly there is no position of moral consciousness which is not liable to be shaken through the exposure of the contradictions inherent in it. These contradictions Hegel designates the " Antinomy of the Moral View of the World." [2] They are founded on the dualism between duty and actuality which makes duty ineffective and inactive.

Now against this dualism a new form of moral spirit rises, namely, Conscience. Conscience emerges as the return, out of the contradictions of dualism, of the moral spirit to itself and its self-certainty as the only source of its conduct. In itself there is no opposition between reason and sensuousness, duty and inclination. It is immediately conscious of the right and good and does it without hesitation. Its duties are its convictions, intentions and motives. The motto here is no longer " I feel that I should do Duty for Duty's sake," but " I have the duty to act according to my conviction, according to my best knowledge and conscience, because it is mine."

1. K. Fischer: *op. cit.*, pp. 406, 407.
2. Hegel's Phän., p. 408, Baillie's Trans., p. 642.

The conscience in question, however, is not the **universal con-**
sciousness of duty which judges all our conduct as to whether it is
conformable to or against duty, but the self-certainty of an individual
fully conscious of his own worth, whose self-determinations, because
they are his own, cannot be otherwise than dutiful. " This conscience
is free (or detached) from every possible content. It absolves itself
from every possible specific duty which would try to pass for a law.
In the strength of the certainty of itself it has the majesty of absolute
self-sufficiency, of absolute authority to bind and to loose." [1] " The
conscience, therefore, in its majestic sublimity or elevation above
any specific law and every content of duty, posits whatever content
there is in its knowledge and willing. It becomes moral genius and
originality, which takes the inner voice of its immediate knowledge
to be a divine voice." [2]

Since conscience is chiefly a matter of personal conviction, which
not everybody has and knows, the truth of it manifests itself not so
much in deed as in the assurance that one fosters such conviction,
in the pronunciation or expression of it, in discourse and talk about
it, and especially in that kindred souls mutually communicate their
convictions and corroborate one another in their conscientiousness which
has nothing to do with the general sense of duty and ordinary morality.
" The spirit and substance of their community are thus the mutual
assurance of their conscientiousness, of their good intentions, the
rejoicing over this reciprocal purity of purpose and the quickening and
refreshment received from the glorious privilege of knowing and of
getting expression, of fostering and cherishing a state so altogether
excellent and desirable." [3]

In this moral self-adulation vanity grows, and the consciousness
prefers indulging itself in judging and discourse to action in order
not to spoil its toilet and stain its purity through contact with
actuality. So out of conscience arises the " beautiful soul " in
its feeble and timid sentimentality which exhales fragrance and

1. Hegel's Phän., p. 418, Baillie's Trans., p. 658.
2. Ibid., p. 422, B. T., p. 664.
3. Ibid., p. 423, B. T., p. 665.

evaporates. To quote Hegel himself: "It lacks the force to externalize itself, the power to give itself embodiment and endure the existence of the same. It lives in the anxiety of staining the splendor of its inner being by action and embodiment. To preserve the purity of its heart it flees from contact with actuality and steadfastly perseveres in a state of impotence to renounce a self which has been pared away to the last point of abstraction and to give itself substantival existence or, in other words, to transform its thought into being and commit itself to absolute distinction. The hollow object, which it produces, now fills it, therefore, with the feeling of emptiness. Its activity consists in yearning; it merely loses itself in becoming an unsubstantial shadowy object, and rising above this loss and falling back on itself, finds itself merely as lost. In this transparent purity of its moments it becomes an unhappy (or sorrow-laden) beautiful soul as it is called; its light dims and dies within it, and it vanishes as a shapeless vapor dissolving itself into thin air." [1]

There is an alternative way of self-expansion open to the conscience which laid its emphasis on personal conviction and trend of willing in place of the notion of duty. This is diametrically opposite to the inactive existence of the beautiful soul just exhibited. That is, it leads through energetic action prompted by private motives to such an opposition against common sense and ordinary moral duty that this conscience, on its own account, appears as capricious, selfish, egoistic, or in a word as a wicked disposition, which, under the mask of conscientious conviction, the show of right and good, plays the hypocrite.

Opposite to this wicked disposition there is a judging and criticizing mind which is spying everywhere after, and ever eager to unmask, selfish and bad intentions. It counts the great men of the world as wicked and bad, because they accomplished their objects in such extraordinary ways that they take the great thing as their own personal affairs and hence it is difficult to draw the line between sacrifice or devotion and self-interest or fame-seeking, honor-coveting, and happiness-pursuing. " From such judgment no act can escape. For ' duty for duty's sake,' the bare purpose, is something unreal. What reality it has lies in the deed of

---

1. Hegel's Phän., p. 425, Baillie's Trans., pp. 667, 668.

some individuality; and the action thereby has in it the aspect of particularity. No hero is a hero to his valet, not, however, because the hero is not a hero, but because the valet is the valet with whom the hero has to do, not as a hero, but as a man who eats, drinks, and dresses, who, in short, appears as a particular individual with certain wants and idiosyncrasies. In the same way there is no act in which that process of judgment cannot oppose the particular aspect of individuality to the universal aspect of the act, and set the valet of morality against the hero who does the act." [1]

Such judgment " is, again, hypocrisy, because it takes this way of judging, not for another fashion of being wicked, but for the correct consciousness of the act. It sets itself up, in its inactuality, in the vanity of knowing well and better, far above the deeds it decries, and wants to find its mere words without deeds taken for an admirable kind of reality." [2] In other words, it does not prove its uprightness and honesty by acts, but pretends to have done so by expressing fine sentiments. Such judgment is in fact just as bad as what (according to its opinion) is the wicked disposition.

Now, if each of the both sides knows its nullity, purifies itself, and reëstablishes the purity of self-consciousness or ego, the opposition dissolves; and there arises, from and on each of the two sides, the reconciliation which Hegel calls " Evil or Wickedness and its Forgiveness." The antithesis is not removed but rather survives in fuller actuality and force; on each side stands the actual knowing, the self-consciousness, the ego, but so, that each, so far from denying, recognizes the other. Now self-consciousness is doubled in the true sense of the word. This mutual recognition is the absolute spirit. " The reconciling affirmation, the ' yes,' with which both egos desist from their existence in opposition, is the existence of the ego expanded into a duality, an ego which remains therein one and identical with itself, and has in its complete relinquishment and its counterpart the certainty of itself." [3]

1. Hegel's Phän., pp. 429, 430, Baillie's Trans., p. 675.
2. *Ibid.*, p. 430, *B. T.*
3. *Ibid.*, p. 434, *B. T.*, p. 682.

CHAPTER IV

THE PHILOSOPHICAL PROPÆDEUTIC, THE ENCYCLOPÆDIA OF PHILOSOPHICAL SCIENCES, AND THE PHILOSOPHY OF RIGHT

1. *The Philosophical Propædeutic*

The Philosophical Propædeutic is a compendium of the lecture notes given by Hegel during the years 1808–1811 at the Gymnasium of Nurenberg. It was edited by Rosenkranz and published in the complete works as volume XVIII. As stated in the Preface, Rosenkranz was of opinion that the Propædeutic forms a significant moment in the development of Hegel. But I think this is perhaps more true of his whole system than of his ethical teaching, seeing that during that period he was occupied chiefly with his " Science of Logic." [1] However, there is something worth noticing in it, even from the standpoint of his ethical teaching. Therefore, a few remarks must be made about it before we can proceed to deal with his later works of ethical importance.

In the introduction [2] Hegel states that the object of his teaching in that course is human will: human will in the form of the relation of particular will to universal will. As will the Spirit takes a practical attitude. Practical attitude differs from the theoretical in that the Spirit as will sets up a determination in its indeterminateness, or, in place of determinations existing in it without its coöperation—i. e., from without, sets another out of itself. The ego appears as practical when the principles of the ego remain no longer as mere inner categories of representing and thinking, but by purposive action step into the external world and acquire for themselves external existence, or in other words, get themselves realized. This is the theory of will Hegel set forth definitely for the first time in his philosophical development.

1. Cf. K. Fischer, *op. cit.*, p. 83.
2. Sections 1–4

In the section on the theory of Duty or morals [1] Hegel differentiates Duty into duty (1) to oneself, (2) to the family, (3) to the State, (4) to Man in general. Among the duties to oneself the most important one is discipline or training, both theoretical and practical. Under the head of theoretical discipline come (1) breadth of learning, in order to be able to appreciate all sorts of relations, actions and things ; (2) definiteness of knowledge so as to be able to differentiate between the essential and unessential ; (3) universality of viewpoint from which one can judge of things in accordance with their true notion ; (4) sense of objectivity without subjective bias.

To the practical discipline belongs prudence and moderation in the satisfaction of natural needs and instincts. Such satisfaction must be restricted within the bounds of necessity. In other words the individual agent must be master of, but not at the mercy of, natural impulses and the seductions of sense. On the other hand he must be absorbed in his occupation. Thus through his efficiency he may push beyond the limits of necessary needs and be in a position to sacrifice something to higher duty.

Hegel's teaching concerning the duties to family and State here is not so detailed as elsewhere ; it is, therefore, better to discuss it in another connection. Among the duties to Man in general,[2] first of all come the duties of Right. Indeed, the moral mood of thinking and behaving passes beyond Right. But righteousness is nevertheless the first duty to be laid as the foundation. There can be noble and magnanimous actions which are without righteousness. They have, then, their ground in self-love and in the feeling of having done something exceptional. In fact, what we can and ought to render to others depends upon the relations in which we stand to them, and upon the particular circumstances in which we find ourselves. The duty of universal love to human beings extends first to those with whom we are in the relation of acquaintance and friendship. The original unity of Man must be spontaneously developed into the closer relations through which definite duties arise.

---

1. See sections 40–42.
2. See sections 59, 60, 66, and 67.

2. *The Encyclopædia of the Philosophical Sciences :*
The Presentation of Hegel's Whole System

The Encyclopædia was published in 1817 when Hegel held the chair of Philosophy at Heidelberg. It was immediateiy preceded by the " Science of Logic " in 1812–1816. This is the second and in a way the most important of the four great works which Hegel himself published. But for our purpose it is out of place to enter upon a discussion of it.

The Encyclopædia is, as Wallace says,[1] the only complete, mature, and authentic statement of Hegel's philosophical system. As every student of Hegel knows, the Hegelian system forms an organic whole. Indeed, such is the close texture of its organization that no part can be isolated without falsification or, at least, distortion. And, as we have seen,[2] Hegel has rightly and strongly insisted, in the very early days of his philosophical inquiry, that no science can be treated independently of the whole system. It is, therefore, necessary for a study of his ethical teaching to acquire a clear conception of the system as a whole, and then to see the ethical doctrine in the light of the whole system. Fortunately, Hegel has furnished us with such an instrument in the Encyclopædia that we can easily achieve our purpose.

In point of content the Encyclopædia is not, as the name might suggest *prima facie,* a mere compendium of separate and single disciplines. On the contrary, it offers a comprehensive exposition of the essential parts of Philosophy in their interconnection (*Zusammenhang*). Adopting Hegelian language, it is concerned with Absolute Reality, or the Idea, in the three phases of Unity, Difference, and Totality or Individuality, which complete its manifestation. Conformably with these phases the work divides itself necessarily into three parts : (1) Logic, (2) the Philosophy of Nature, and (3) the Philosophy of Spirit (*Geist*).

The first, mainly an abridged edition of the " Science of Logic," is an investigation of the organic system of the characteristic forms of

1. The Logic of Hegel, p. IX.
2. See before, pp. 1, 2, and 6.

thought, that is, the Categories. Starting with the most abstract, the Logic shows that, owing to their instability, due to finitude, they pass over by a natural dialectic process into more adequate expressions till, ultimately, concrete forms are evolved wherein the complete totality of the Idea can find expression.

In Hegel's view the Idea being the "unity of knowledge and reality" is logically known within the "medium of thought." Its claim to objective validity remains to be proved. Accordingly, it must realize or manifest itself in a realm which is, somehow, other than pure Thought. Hence the Philosophy of Nature. In Nature the Idea particularizes itself, passing over into the phases of time, space, and phenomenal existence. This particularization, giving rise to new possibilities, leads on to a necessary re-integration through the several forms of organic life till, at length, the finite Spirit culminates in Man. That is to say, Man can justify a claim to be regarded as the final expression of Nature, because through him alone is the interpretation of Nature possible. And as soon as interpretation begins to develop, we have the Philosophy of Spirit.

In this Part of the Encyclopædia Hegel exhibits the entire process of spiritual (*geistiges*) life. As usual with him, it differentiates itself into three moments : (1) Subjective Spirit, (2) Objective Spirit, (3) Absolute Spirit. The first deals with the soul anthropologically after the fashion then common in Germany, elaborated later by Hegel's follower, Feuerbach ; with the phenomenology of Spirit, to the examination of which his first great work had been devoted ; and with what is to-day usually relegated to empirical psychology. The second, by far the most important for our present inquiry, presents the objective manifestation of Spirit as traceable in legal relations, conscience, and social life ; while the third deals with Absolute Spirit, Spirit as its own object, revealing itself in æsthetic appreciation, religious meditation, and pure speculative activity.

Now it is easy to see that this procedure indicates the precise place held by Ethics in the Hegelian system. The ethical life, as we take it in this treatise, is the revelation of Spirit as it operates in the social medium supplied by group relations. The province of ethical

Spirit lies between Subjective Spirit and Absolute Spirit. In other words, Spirit comes out of itself, abandoning whatever mere self-regard it may have, and blossoms in relation to the general movement of all Spirits, these in turn being viewed as the vehicles of a Universal or Absolute Spirit. It is still bound by external forms, but these are now of such a character as to partake of its own nature, so that the interference is apparent rather than real. In the first Sub-Division of Division II, Hegel discusses Abstract Right, where the conditions seem to partake most of externality. The second Sub-Division deals with Morality of Conscience, as the completion of purpose and intention, where, evidently, the inner movement and the outer are conjoined. For purpose and intention, whatever they may be in themselves, are dependent upon conditions for realization. In the third Sub-Division these two unite, and we find ourselves in the realm of Ethicality. The main phases here are the Family, Civic Society, and the State. Hegel's thesis, so commonly misapprehended to-day, may be stated as follows. The ethical life of man is the result of the interpretation of Man by Man. This produces views, dispositions, manners, disciplines, morals, customs, conventions, institutions, and the like. These again are what they are thanks to the presence of a common or unitary Spirit. Man, the individual, shares in this Spirit and, in one way, is moulded by it. On the other hand, this Spirit must be manifested in individual men. Accordingly, the problem comes to be one, not of the individual or of society as such, but of the internal principle of relation binding the individual and the pervasive Spirit into a single whole. The right of the individual against society, and the abrogation of this right by society are alike abstractions. The question is of the controlling principle whereby these movements occur, and of the implications of these movements in the gradual development of this principle.

3. *The Philosophy of Right (Rechtsphilosophie):*

A Part of the Philosophy of Spirit

"The Philosophy of Right" is an elaborate discussion of the positions presented in the second part of the Philosophy of Spirit, i.e., the Objective Spirit. It is thus little more than an expansion of that portion. No doubt this elaboration raises new problems. But the main principle stands without alteration.

From Hegel's own Preface we can gather that he did not originally plan to issue " the Philosophy of Right " as an independent work. The motive which prompted him to detach a portion of the "Philosophy of Spirit " and to elaborate it into a separate volume was perhaps a wish to respond to the enthusiasm of his Berlin audience. They had welcomed warmly his brilliant lectures on the fundamental principles of political, social, and moral institutions, which were so urgently needed at that moment for the salvation of Germany. In any case, it is certain that Hegel himself never took " the Philosophy of Right " as a complete self-contained Ethical system. One or two things indicate this very clearly.

In the first place Religion had been so prominent a factor in the constitution of Hegel's mind and temperament that his whole philosophical system tended, as some complain, to " theologism." [1] Particularly in regard to Ethics, Hegel does indeed consider religion as absolutely essential. In the Encyclopædia [2] he has gone so far as to say that "Religion is the very substance of the moral life and of the State . . . the State rests on the ethical sentiment and this on the religious." His notion of Ethics and the moral life was such that, had he taken " the Philosophy of Right " as a self-sufficing ethical system, he would have devoted a sub-division or, at least, an important section to the discussion of religion. But in point of fact he only slightly touched on its relation to the State in a note, and in an addendum to section 270, where the main subject at issue is not religion.

Secondly, " the Philosophy of Right " traces the dialectic development of the several forms of the right of the free will, and shows that these forms, being finite and unstable, must lead into the realm of Absolute Spirit wherein the limitations of finite spirit or Objective Spirit are transcended. But of this realm of Absolute Spirit Hegel here in " the Philosophy of Right " contents himself with a bare mention only.

1. The validity or invalidity of such criticism does not concern us here.
2. Section 552.

It is quite inconceivable that so thorough and systematic a thinker as Hegel could allow himself to publish an unfinished work. This shows clearly that he has taken for granted that "the Philosophy of Right" is not meant to be a complete ethical system. It merely treats of Spirit in its objective aspect, while a complete ethical system must extend into the realm of Absolute Spirit. Of course this realm contains more than what is ethical; but the ethical cannot be complete apart from this realm.

As the part which deals with the "Objective Spirit" and the "Philosophy of Right" are substantially the same, we may treat of them just as if they were only two editions of one work. In fact, Kuno Fischer in his "*Geschichte der neuern Philosophie*" has done so. In the following chapters the present writer also will adopt this method. Not only are there positive reasons which indicate that this is the proper way to treat the subject; there are also negative considerations which require this method of treatment still more imperatively. For we know that some critics used to complain that Hegel's "Philosophy of Right" is too pedestrian to be an ethical work. For it deals mainly with the commonplace problems of daily life, but lacks the deeper elements of inner experience, such as mental discipline, æsthetic contemplation, aspiration, meditation, purely speculative activities, or pious, lofty, and holy states of mind. Such criticism is in itself perfectly right and can be met only by pointing to the fact that the "*Rechtsphilosophie*" is only an elaboration of a partial study, that dealing with Objective Spirit, in "the Philosophy of Spirit." It is preceded by a part dealing with Subjective Spirit and succeeded by another dealing with Absolute Spirit. A work elaborated from such a section of a larger system can be judged only as fitting into the place it originally occupied in the whole organism; and, again, it must be judged according as it performs the function assigned to it; we must not expect a part to bear the burden of the whole system. In other words, "the Philosophy of Right" is not to stand alone. It must be referred back to the whole scheme of the "Encyclopædia"; otherwise it will be misapprehended. Unless this attitude is taken, all criticism of Hegel is bound to be unfair.

CHAPTER V

OBJECTIVE SPIRIT AND THE PHILOSOPHY OF RIGHT

In the last chapter we have seen the place of ethics in the whole philosophical system of Hegel; we have seen that the ethical life, as presented in the second division, the division on "Objective Spirit," of "the Philosophy of Spirit" which is the third part of the "Encyclopædia," and elaborated in "the Philosophy of Right," follows upon the preliminary or "Subjective" stages of Spirit. In other words, the external facts of ethical life presuppose (1) the fixation of the disciplined powers and habits of the body, (2) the development of consciousnes through struggle with objects forward to an assurance of adjustment with the world, (3) the acquisition of a free mind in the sense in which mind is employed by psychology in the proper sense.

Now, according to Hegel, the term "free" mind implies its possession of Will. In the Introduction to "the Philosophy of Right" Hegel gives us an elaborate theory of will. In the following pages this theory of will will be discussed at length. For the present moment we shall proceed to set forth the objective manifestations of Will.

Will is a capacity to seek satisfaction in objects and activities. Hence the "free" mind, the individual agent possessing will, is capable of taking steps to realize itself. This process, as exhibited in "the Philosophy of Spirit," and "the Philosophy of Right," involves three stages or aspects, as follows: Abstract Right, Morality, and Ethicality (*Sittlichkeit*). Although these stages imply different objective facts, they constitute a single process. The different manifestations are not to be considered as successive developments in time. Doubtless, it is true, that, in primitive communities, Abstract Right preponderates. Nevertheless, even there the factors of Conscience and Ethicality are at work, although they find inadequate expression. Similarly, even in advanced societies, Abstract Right survives and often impedes both Conscience and Ethicality.

50

A. *Abstract Right*

At first Will is undeveloped, merely potential; in other words, the capacity of will is unexercised, and remains "formal." In this stage of undeveloped freedom, therefore, will is as good as non-existent. It is confronted, and therefore limited, by an entire universe of alien nature, wherewith it has as yet no connection. On the other hand, the bare fact of will must consist in, and spring from, an activity whereby this limitation is annulled, and will reaches a measure of objective power. Thus, in order to acquire objective validity, will must first of all actualize itself by appropriating the natural order that stands over against it. The *right* to objectification is derived from "formal" will — will as yet without consideration of its formation or its relation to environment, and therefore "abstract." Accordingly, the sphere of Abstract Right includes whatever is *immediately* contained in (or follows from) objectification. In Hegel's view, three manifestations occur here: Property; Contract; Justice and Crime.

1. *Property*

Property is to be described as objectified will; that is, it is an object into which I have introduced my will, thus making it an attribute of self. Seeing that I have thus identified myself with it, anyone who touches it thereby touches me, intrudes on my living substance, that is, my will. By the possession of property the " free " will takes the first step towards its own objective validity. Thus the necessity of the existence of property, or of the appropriation of objects external to his " formal " will, is inseparable from man's development beyond mere subjective possibility. It is the initial step towards actuality.

Possession is effected (*a*) partly by physical occupation; (*b*) partly by formative work ; (*c*) partly by mere marking or labelling — the affixing of some sign of ownership. In these ways the ' thing ' no longer exists for itself, but for something else (' another '). Therefore property is not fully such unless it is treated as instrumental, i. e., for use or consumption. This is inseparable from true proprietorship. Similarly, property may be relinquished by its possessor. Seeing that it is mine only in so far as I put my will into it, I can abandon my dominion, delivering the object to others. This indicates that so far the 'thing' remains external: my free will is objectified in it only by accident. Accordingly, the connection is not irrevocable and may be broken *at will* (another exercise of will). Primarily, in property it is a single will that is related to things. But these same things are connected with other things, with possible or actual properties. This raises the question of the relation of will to will, and leads forthwith to the sphere of Contract.

2. *Contract*

Contract is a process which attempts the unification of different wills. Property which is thus held implies the sanction of common consent, with severalty of parties. In short, my will is not actually objectified in the object unless my *de facto* possession is recognized by another. The essence of the matter is to be found in a "dialectic" process, generating a contradiction describable as follows: I am and can remain an owner only to the extent to which I can identify myself with the will of another, and therefore cease to be a *mere* owner. This contradiction is traceable to the fact that the very intention of Contract is the identification of different (and therefore implicitly opposed) wills, in such a way that their particularities can be at the same time formatively transcended *and* ideally retained as component factors. Consequently, in virtue of Contract, both parties emerge, after *surrender* of property, in *possession* of property plus security — that is, with enhanced "concreteness" of will. Moreover, although Contract, with its stipulation and subsequent obligation, implies more than mere promise, it nevertheless proceeds from arbitrary choice of the parties, and to this extent expresses the intrinsic will of the community only in relation to a particular, that is, an arbitrary affair. The development must proceed further.

3. *Wrong or Cirme*

Seeing, then, that the "common" will incident to Contract is not intrinsically or essentially universal, " it contains no guarantee of its own agreement with the universal rational will or essential justice, nor any assurance of that good faith on the part of the contracting parties on which it must depend for its own maintenance. Under these circumstances nothing but accident can protect it from being or becoming essential wrong." [1] Wrongs may be classified as (1) Unconscious or Unintentional or Civil Wrong; (2) Fraud; (3) Violence and Crime. This analysis, it may be noted, serves to show that Hegel's idealism is sound precisely to the extent to which it is based on " brute " or unpleasant realism.

Civil Wrong ensues when claims to the same thing come into collision. It originates because each person maintains what *he* believes to be right. Still, it negates only the particular will of the adversary ; the general legal right is respected. Contentions of this kind furnish the sphere of civil actions. The object in dispute goes to him whose claim the general will decides to be right, and therefore valid.

Fraud is the substitution of simulated for actual right. The element of *conscious* intention renders it the second stage of Wrong. The particular will is not necessarily injured here, for the wrong doer may succeed in inducing his victim to believe that fair treatment has been given. On the contrary, universal Right is injured fatally, for form is put forward as substance, to conceal the invasion of Right. Thus, while no punishment is prescribed for unintentional worng, it is prescribed for Fraud, because Right cannot but be specifically injured.

Violence or constraint is produced by the projection of my will into an external thing. My property may be made the means whereby violence is done to my will, or through my property I may be coerced against my will. Therefore, as Hegel urges, violence must be annulled by violence, since it is essentially self-destructive. In short, a second coercion must abrogate the first, and this, not simply on grounds of conditional legality, but of moral necessity.

Elaborating this point, Hegel sets forth his classical discussion of Punishment. His fundamental position is that punishment is intrinsically just alike to society and to the individual criminal. It does

---

1. G. S. Morris, Hegel's Philosophy of History, p. 21.

not merely ensue upon the nature of the crime, but is an explicit development of what was implicit in the will of the criminal. Paradoxically, it must be regarded as a definite form of the development of his own freedom. For his action, being that of a rational will, implies an element of universality. That is, he implicitly recognizes his act as a possible law of action for all, and so he cannot but be judged and treated according to this *common* factor. Hence Punishment is essentially retributive. Crime is no bare accidental evil, but a violation of ultimate justice or right. It *must* be negated. Consequently, punishment does not find its justification in its deterrent influence nor in any prospective good to the criminal. No doubt it has also a preventive and reformatory effect; but the intrinsic ground of it is the right of the criminal to retribution; and this demands due punishment of the crime. [1]

B. *Morality*

In the realm of Abstract Right the individual counts only as a conventional person. But, when the sphere of morality is reached, he becomes inwardly free and is properly characterized as a " subject " — a will so reflected into itself as to acquiesce only in what springs from the Good Will; or, what is the same thing, only in what fulfils its own principle. The legal order is but the first necessary step on the way to freedom. But the will continually collides with law, which proves inadequate to realize its purpose completely. This conflict recurs in history; ancient Stoicism and modern Protestantism furnish striking examples. The classical expression of it, however, is to be found in the Kantian doctrine of the Good Will, as formulated in the aphorism: " Nothing can possibly be conceived in the world or out of it which can be called good without qualification except a good will." [2] The right of this Good Will presents three aspects: Purpose and Responsibility; Intention and Well-being; Good and Conscience.

1. *Purpose and Responsibility*

In Purpose the Rational Will proposes to effect alterations in the external world through its own agency and according to its idea

1. Cf. McTaggart : Studies in Hegelian Cosmology, Chap. V.
2. Grund, z. Meta. d. Sitten, section I.

(*Vorstellung*).   It therefore holds itself *responsible* for the change. Unfortunately, unforeseen consequences may (and usually do) accompany the alterations.   For these subjective will by no means holds itself responsible as part of its conduct (*Handlung*), although they were elicited by its act (*That*).   In other words, it claims to be held responsible merely for the consequences that lay within its knowledge; that is, were involved in the original design.   Now, while it is true that many consequences are beyond calculation, it is also true that a universal and necessary element attaches to the simplest act.   This is part of its intention, no matter how completely implicit.   Hence purpose necessarily passes over to intention.

2.   *Intention and Well-being*

Intention may be described as purpose proceeding from a rational will, but involving the universal as well as the individual aspect.   It is therefore dependent upon insight.   When this insight is wanting, as in children or imbeciles, real purpose based on universal principle is excluded.   But what is true completely of these defectives holds true in a measure of all men.   For the intention of the individual cannot well be co-extensive with the universal implications of his act ; for what he has are particular aims peculiar to *a* human being.   These are concerned with well-being, or subjective freedom, and possess relative justification. The needs, interests, inclinations, convictions, desires, hopes, and aspirations of the agent do find expression therein, and, to this extent, have their own rightness.   But they may not be indulged uncondi- tionally, for each must respect the well-being of others and of the communal whole.   A good intention does not justify a wrong deed,[1] because the subjective element conflicts with the objective, and the estimate of the deed remains superficial.   But this very contingency of intention leads the individual to seek a principle of justification for his act. That is he is driven to formulate a universal in defence of *his* particulars, in order that *his* personality may not be violated.   Hence conscience.

---

1.   On the other hand, to find fault with the personal aspects of the illustrious deeds of great individuals is equally unjustifiable. See the preceding No., pp. 45, 46 and K. Fischer, *op. cit.*, pp. 705, 706.

3. *The Good and Conscience*

The Good is the ideal unity of the notion (*Begriff*) of universal will with a particular will. Being the ultimate purpose of the ethical world it is really inseparable from what seems to be a mere subjective will. Accordingly, well-being has worth and dignity only in so far as insight grasps the notion of the Good. Therefore the particular subject must be subordinated to the purpose of the universal. Briefly, well-being is not a good apart from universal right, while universal right is not the Good without well-being. Even so, the Good is as yet no more than an *abstract* universal. That is to say, it has not been brought into relation with the actual situation in such a way as to render the particular will conformable to it. Felt as an imperative, it is nevertheless fatally vague and indeterminate. For instance, the Kantian maxim " Duty for Duty's sake," affords no immanent guide to duty in a given case. It must borrow from some principle already established ; only in so far as the rights of property and life are *already* presupposed, for example, can theft and murder be designated crime. Thus, by self-deception, any formal maxim could be twisted to support any act, moral or immoral.[1]

Consequently, the abstract, formal notion of Good, as determined by conscience, necessitates the delegation of the determining function to accidental units. The norm of action falls within *subjective* conviction, known popularly as Conscience. Now, while this is an element in the realization of freedom, it is no more than an element. For private conscience is liable to whim, fancy, caprice, and even to ridiculous error. This lack of objective content is apt to produce anarchism, sophistry, hypocrisy ; and these are worse than mere blind acquiescent submission to law.[2] Genuine conscience, on the contrary, embodies a factor drawn

---

1. See before pp. 8, 9.
2. See before, pp. 39 f. Hegel's theory of evil demands mention here. Briefly it is as follows: Moral evil originates in the ambiguity between subjective conscience and objective good. Evil ensues when the former is elevated to supremacy over, or is immediately identified with, the latter. In the naïve stage (of undeveloped universality) people are neither bad nor positively good : they are merely unconscious. When particularity is differentiated, in the stage of reflection, they are liable to be both good and evil. But thanks to the nature of particularity, the good is not complete, nor is the evil absolute. Not till the stage of completion (Individuality) is reached can the good attain such absoluteness that evil may be transcended.

from the objective validity of established principle. It accepts voluntarily the current, explicit virtues and duties, recognizing them as necessary, because essential to its own growth and to the best life. It does not thereby forfeit its own right of insight, but mediates it through the realized system. This mediation, involving the union of subjective knowledge with objective socialization, is to be attained only in the stage of Ethicality (*Sittlichkeit*).

C. *Ethicality*

Ethicality, as Hegel explains, is "the Idea of freedom," [1] or "the perfection of the Objective Spirit." [2] It might be termed the living Good, because it attains knowledge, volition, and actuality by and through the activity of self-consciousness. On the other hand, in the Ethicality self-consciousness finds its own "absolute ground," "the underlying essence of its own very being and nature," "its absolute final aim." Thus *Sittlichkeit* comes to be "the notion of freedom developed into the present existing world, and into the nature of self-consciousness." Here particular wills and universal will attain unity. Consciousness manifests itself in such a way that each "moment" identifies itself with the totality and finds in this totality its ground and content. Hence abstract good is replaced by concrete principle. In short, the differences are unified in an articulated whole of *ethos* and institutions, elevated above subjective opinion and personal inclination. Principles have authority and force here, because for the individual they embody his own selfhood, nay, reveal this on a higher level. They are not alien, for the spirit (*Geist*) bears witness to itself. In union with them a larger, freer, completer life is gained. This consummation is effected, first by faith and trust ; then by conviction or insight; finally by clear intellectual grasp of immanent meaning. The generality or vagueness of the "pure" Good Will gives way to a thoroughly systematized conception, such that the relation between individual particulars and the universal Spirit becomes plain.

1. Rechtsphil., section 142.
2. Encycl., section 513.

True, the individual does not lose his individuality, but he finds himself substantially determined to action by duties, which derive authority from free obligation.   That is to say, he has arrived at the point where he grasps the identity of duty with Right.   He realizes that he has rights only in proportion as he fulfils obligations ; so these duties, far from being limitations, are opportunities—*the* opportunities for self-realization.   The impulses of the natural will, with their caprice, have been moralized and rendered stable by liberation from indeterminate choice.   Hence, for the first time, man reckons himself free.

From this point of view *Sittlichkeit* does the work of Law and Moral Will, in practice and theory alike.   For, besides revealing the principle of unity immanent in society, it affirms human freedom in the three chief aspects of common life : the Family, Civic Society, and the Political Organization of the State.   Externally, these three present different groups of facts, different modes of association ; inwardly, they are moods or dispositions of one indivisible spirit (*Geist*).[1]   There is no self-sufficient family without the civic community, nor is the civic community possible without some form of State.   On the other hand, no State can accomplish its ends apart from domestic and civic institutions. The predominance of any one is temporary.   Further development adjusts the balance ; otherwise society would commit suicide.[2]

1. *The Family*

The reality of spirit receives *immediate* substantial realization in the Family, which is based on the feeling of love.[3]   Hence the unity occupies the first place, the individual being a member, but not an independent person.   When the family is dissolved the person becomes independent in the sense of receiving what may be apportioned to him of the external

---

1. Cf. the Philosophical Theory of the State, B. Bosanquet, pp. 268 f.
2. See before, pp. 32, 33.
3. For Hegel Love implies my consciousness of unity with another.   Its first phase is that I no longer wish to be independent, isolated, self-sufficing and that, if I remained thus separate, I should be defective and incomplete.   Its second phase is that I renounce my exclusive existence, thereby uniting myself with another.

goods, thanks to his membership in the unity. The Family develops itself in three phases : Marriage, Means or Property, Education of children and eventual dissolution of the group.

a. *Marriage*

Marriage implies, first, the elemental sex-relation common to all animals. But, in man, because he is a spiritual being, natural instinct has come to be transformed and illuminated by the touch of self-conscious love. A spiritual bond supervenes upon the natural. Therefore, for Hegel, marriage is to be described as legal-ethical love, that is, emotional life mediated through the common stock of intelligence as embodied in ethico-legal institutions. It is not a mere sexual relation, nor a union based on fluctuating sentiment; still less is it a civil contract, as Kant held. It is rather personality mediated through personality and so enriched. No doubt, as Hegel admits, it contains accidental elements, such as temporary inclination, and the plans of parents. Nevertheless, these very phases are themselves part of a larger order, and serve to minimize the contingency of sudden passion, which so easily leads to tragedy. On the other hand, marriage for the sake of political or similar ends tends to defeat itself, because the unity is exploited for a purpose beyond itself. Accordingly, the real point of the relationship consists in the free consent of two to be hereafter one, to resign their natural isolation for this moralizing unity. It is a species of self-limitation which, like all reasonable sacrifice, results in self-development. For the family is a veritable school of ethical culture, opening up higher aims and bestowing fuller individuality. The ethical element is traceable to the socialized disposition which reduces natural impulse to a mode, at the same time elevating the spiritual bond to supreme significance. Thus the family becomes a single person, giving reverence to its own spirit, as the *Penates* and other similar symbols show. The unity is " accidental " in so far as it is part of a greater whole. Therefore social celebration, or rather sanction, is necessary to make sure that the union is recognized by the community. The legal or ecclesiastical " proceedings " are thus significant, not in themselves, but as signs of seriousness and solemnity.

b. *Family Means (Property or Fortune)* [1]

Being a moral person the family needs a basis of substantial reality, to be found in a certain permanent means or fortune ; otherwise it cannot endure. The abstract right to property, which tends to keep persons separate, is now transformed into an ethical activity for a common weal. Family property is thus based on common right, even if the family head has a superior power of disposition. For, through marriage of a scion, a new family arises and, in Hegel's view, property is vitally connected with this and exists for the common good.

c. *Education of Children and Dissolution of the Family*

Children incarnate and objectify the love which lies at the basis of the original family, which is thus given a new and independent existence. In short, the unity is further actualized in fresh spiritual being. Hence, children have the right to receive support and education at the family charge. On the other hand, parents have the right to require of the children subordination to the common interests of the group, so instilling into them something beyond mere separate selfhood. In accordance with this the aim of education is twofold; first, to elicit the ethical nature of the child as far as possible, establishing the state of mind indispensable to a healthy moralized life ; secondly, to lift the child out of natural simplicity and dependence into free personality, thus enabling him to quit the natural unity of the family and to carry it on for himself.

The dissolution of the family may be effected by divorce. This is an unavoidable contingency, seeing that marriage always contains an element of subjectivity, which exposes it to accidents. But, in such event, a third authority must intervene to uphold the common ethical fabric, and above all, to restrain mere caprice. Normal dissolution ensues when the children, having attained free personality, proceed to found new families away from the old home. Another kind of normal dissolution occurs when, by the death of parents, children inherit the family wealth. In respect to inheritance, Hegel considers the rights of

---

1. See before, p. 18.

children as more substantial and ethical than any other claim. At the same time, he excludes special favors for special aims, such as are illustrated, for example, by the custom of primogeniture.

2.   *The Civic Community*

The transformations of the family take place in a quite natural way, chiefly through expansion into the sphere of the Civic Community. There the family tends to maintain a separate existence, and therefore to be related to others *externally*. Here we find a new aspect of differentiation, where group-interest, *almost individualistic*, dominates consciousness. Hence the Civic Community is to be described as the " State External" or the " Police State." It implies the *mechanical* adjustment of conflicting self-interests according to a universal law, giving security and protection. Here the law is a task-master, a limitation, because the tendency of the Civic Community is to seek property first, socialization being secondary. Hence, too, the Law is also a schoolmaster, inculcating social duty and thus directing men towards a more substantial freedom. Viewed in this way the Civic Community reveals three phases; the System of Wants; the Administration of Justice; Police and Corporation.

a.   *The System of Wants*

Subjective wants are particular moods of particular persons. They acquire objective reality by means of (1) external things and (2) active labor, which is the connecting link between subject and object. Human wants and the means for their satisfaction are manifold. This follows from the differentiation of wants and the parallel refinement of means. These complexities necessitate a set of relations between persons such as to facilitate mutual satisfaction. This universal element socializes the several abstract wants and means, rendering them concrete. The instrument for preparation of the means of satisfaction is labor, which is formative through and through, because it appropriates natural things and adjusts them to ends. Specialization of needs results in division of labor, rendering it easier, more skillful and productive. But, on the other hand, this deprives men of self-sufficiency and grafts them into the social fabric. Thus a commercial system is constructed, wherein all are mutually dependent. But this by no means implies equality. For persons are not born with uniform equipment, such as aptitude, talent, capital, etc. Hence, there is necessarily diversity of contribution, with consequent diversity of distribution of wealth. As a result the whole is divided into groups or "*Stände*." These are: "the substantial '*Stand*' (agriculturalists); the formative '*Stand*' (artisans); the universal '*Stand*' (intellectuals and governors). Determination of the '*Stand*' of an individual depends, as has been suggested, upon his gifts, training and other circumstances. Nevertheless the final and essential factor lies in a man's view of life and in his power of will. Here subjectivity and free choice find their right place, resulting in honor and dignity.

b. *Administration of Justice*

The purpose of this is the protection of the rights of *all* persons to exchange goods, and to serve for the satisfaction of their wants. In this sphere implicit right becomes explicit and is constituted by and for consciousness through universal, authoritative law. By means of this determination right or justice becomes positive or legal right. But this inevitably brings in something external and particular; law thus fails to express the universal with complete adequacy. Therefore private choice or some other arbitrary factor may make entrance, so that statute law may come to be at actual variance with ethical right. On the other hand, unwritten law still presents a wide field of autonomy, option and opinion Legislation thus always faces a dilemma. It ought to formulate the universal principle into definite laws in order to eliminate the danger of caprice and ambiguity. But by the nature of the case no law expresses the universal principle adequately, and consequently the element of indecision cannot be altogether eliminated.[1] Hence codification is requisite, in order that the

---

1. Cf. Encyc., section 529.

universal or intelligible factor may be displayed clearly, alike in regard to what has been attained and in regard to what is still in process of development. The public court of justice derives its sanction from the universal will, in so far as it manifests a fuller revelation of individual will. On this, too, reposes the possibility of justifying punishment. The community, consciously or unconsciously, stands behind the judicial decisions to support them.

c. *Police and Corporation*

By the former term is meant State-regulation and supervision; by the latter trade-societies. The aim of State-regulation is to secure the general conditions under which individuals may obtain what they need. Exchange of goods is no merely private affair, but a matter of common interest. There may be oftentimes over-production, shortage, emergencies, miscarriages, as well as intentional adulteration of goods; or unreasonable luxury may occur, due to caprice. All these phenomena may result in disturbance. The community has a right to intervene here, with official regulation, inspection, supervision, public provision or undertaking, and so on. Trade-societies originate in differentiation of function. Every member of the civic community belongs by his vocation to a '*Stand*' or estate.' By acquiring solidarity with his fellows, the particular aim of the individual is universalized to some extent through common purpose, as in the corporation. "In this he finds his honor or recognition, a definite standard of life (apart from which he is apt to assert himself by aimless extravagance for want of recognized respectability), a standard of work, insurance against misfortune and (while he is a candidate for admission) the means of technical education."[1] As the family is the first basis of the State, so the corporation constitutes the second. "It is the very root of ethical connection between the private and the general interest, and the State should see to it that this root holds as strongly as possible."[2]

1. B. Bosanquet, The Philosophical Theory of the State, p. 279.
2. *Ibid.*

3. *The State*

The State is the actualization of the Ethical Spirit. It is the substantial will, knowing and thinking, and thus realizing a certain type of life. The external force and machinery for the maintenance and adjustment of the rights and purposes of individuals are secondary; they are no more than means to the actualization of the real *inner spirit* of the State, instruments to attain the final end of its entire structure. On the other hand, the self-consciousness of the ethical disposition of individuals finds its congenial freedom only in the organization of the state. The root of duty to the commonwealth lies here. The individual cannot of himself live an ethical life; participation in the life of the nation-group is necessary. Hence the actualization of the ethical whole is necessarily national. Although a national state may be defective in many ways, and violate right principles, it always contains the essential elements of its existence if it belongs to the class of developed States. But, since it is easier to detect shortcomings than to grasp the positive meaning, men readily fall into the mistake of dwelling so much on special aspects as to overlook internal organic character. The State is not a work of art. The bad behavior of its members may disfigure it in many ways. But the most deformed man, the criminal, the invalid, and the cripple, are still living men. The positive element, the life, remains in spite of all defects.

The idea of the State has (a) immediate actuality in the individual and particular state. As a self-concerned organism it is the national constitution or internal State-organization or polity. (b) As external organization or polity it passes over into relations with other States. This gives rise to international law. And (c) as universal idea or kind it has absolute authority over individual states. For thus the spirit of humanity gives itself reality in the process of universal history and is the absolute judge over single states.

a. *National Constitution or Internal Polity*

In the State, or the actuality of concrete freedom, or the ethical sphere, all personal *individuality* and *particular interests* (found in the family and civic society) are united with the *universal*, the *common good* of the nation. This occurs partly through individuals recognizing in thought and deed this universal as being their own substantial spirit, and expending their energies for it as for their own final end. But, on the other hand, the State manifests the principle that my obligation to the *substantial* is likewise the characteristic form of the existence of my particular freedom; that is, in the State duty and right are united. The individual must in one way or another find his own interests and satisfaction in his performance of duty. Thus the common good becomes his particular interest. The State, as contrasted with particular rights *per se* (particular good, of the individual, the family, and the " *Stand* "), is an external necessity. But on the other hand it is also the indwelling end of these things and is strong in its union of the universal end with the particular interests of individuals, families, and " *Stände* "; otherwise it will be a castle built in the air. [1]

The *institutions* and laws of the State have their ground in, and are the manifestation and reflection of, the ethical spirit of the nation. They make up the mood of life of the nation and determine the temper of the individual citizens towards the State. They are the reason of the nation, developed and actualized in particular forms. Thus they involve an intrinsic union of freedom and necessity. But institutions and laws are impersonal and unconscious. They contain in themselves no germ of development. They are the phenomena and product of a public spirit which they presuppose; and this therefore is the true substance of the State.

As subjective substantiality the Idea of the State or the ethical spirit of the nation, forms *political disposition ;* and, as objective, it makes the political State proper and *constitution.* This political disposition is generally termed *patriotism.* Genuine patriotism is manifested by activities in harmony with, and for the sake of, the type of life which is willed by the nation and embodied in the institu-

---

1. See before, pp. 32, 33.

tions of the State. It is this confidence in the State which primarily attains to more or less intelligent insight. By patriotism is frequently understood merely a readiness to submit to exceptional sacrifice or do exceptional acts. But, in reality, it is that disposition which is accustomed to regard the common weal or the type of life willed by the nation as its substantial basis and the final purpose of all activity. This consciousness is kept in contact with the routine of ordinary life, and upon it the readiness to submit to exceptional effort is based. But as men find it easier to be magnanimous than to be merely righteous, they easily persuade themselves they possess this heroic patriotism in order to spare themselves the burden and trouble of the true disposition and to excuse the lack of it. [1]

Political constitution is the articulation or organization of the State-power. It is the political disposition given definite content by the development of the Idea into its differences which are objectively actualized. These differences are the various functions, affairs and activities of the State. By means of them the universal uninterruptedly manifests itself. However, the universal is none the less self-contained, since it is already presupposed in its own productive process, which posits distinctions in itself and there circulates and articulates itself. The constitution provides for the determination of rights, i. e., of liberties in general, while laws provide for the means of the actualization of them.

The *guarantee* of a constitution (i. e., the necessity that the laws be reasonable, and their enforcement assured) lies in the collective spirit of the nation and also in the actual organization and development of that principle in *suitable* institutions. The nexus between the collective spirit in its self-consciousness and the same in its actuality is inseparable. The constitution presupposes the consciousness of the collective spirit, while the spirit does not exist without a constitution, for in the actual spirit alone lies a definite consciousness of its principles. " The question, To whom belongs the power to *make a constitution ?* is the same as the

---

1. Cf. before, p. 44.

question, Who has to make the spirit of a nation?" What is called 'making' a 'constitution' is "a thing that has never happened in history, just as little as the making of a code of laws." Constitution and laws only "develop from the national spirit, identically with that spirit's own development, and runs through at the same time with it the grades of formation and the alternations required by its concept."[1] If you have a multitude new to each other in some extra-political region, they must adopt a constitution before they can make one.

The function of the head of the State is to secure the objectivity of the spiritual unity and to consummate the work of the several branches of the government. It is "the dot on the i." The division of the powers of the State into several branches does not impair the living unity; they are functions distinct but not independent of one another. Sovereignity consists in "the relation in which each factor of the constitution stands to the whole. That is to say, it resides only in the organized whole acting for an organized whole."[2] The function of the *executive* (including judiciary and police) is to develop, preserve, and apply the existing laws, regulations, establishments for common ends, and the like. A certain training, aptitude, and skill determine the selection of individuals to fill these offices. Natural personality or birth should exclude none.

The *legislature* has to supervise the laws and internal affairs of universal interest. This function is itself a part of the constitution. Within this capacity lie the laws of private right in general, the rights of societies and corporations, and also universal institutions and indirectly the whole of the constitution. The principal element in the legislature is formed by the representatives of the different "*Stände*"; but the executive may give advice concerning the detailed facts, while the function of the head of the State is to give the final decision and promulgation.

The assembly of the deputies of the "*Stände*" is to be divided into *two chambers*. The representative Chamber is liable to adopt accidental

1. Hegel's Encycl., section 540.
2   Bosanquet: Phil. Theory of State, p. 282.

decisions made on the spur of the moment. Hence it is expedient to place the second chamber in a position to mediate between the " *Stände* " and the government.

Deputies or representatives should be acquainted with the particular needs and interests of the constituency represented, and with such grievances as specially call for redress. They should therefore be chosen from among the leading people of the same *Stand*, so that they can directly present the point of view of the represented. A representative, in short, is not one person taking the place of another. Rather is he the person standing for the interests and assuming the responsibility actually present in himself, a trustee.

Above all, representation must be based on social unity, not on geographical area. That is to say, it is of organized bodies or interests rather than of indefinite masses of individuals. The former only have concrete opinions and intelligent will. They can realize their interests, and express their view in a right and orderly way. On the contrary the latter, being mere heaps of atoms, have neither definite view nor tangible interests. A representative of such a constituency has nothing to represent ; if he pretended to stand for or against anything his determination would be wayward and arbitrary and his utterance would tend to over-statement.

" Publicity of discussion in the assembly of the ' *Stände* ' is the great means of civic education. It is not in the least true that every one knows what is for the good of the State, and has only to go down to the Chamber to utter it. It is in the work of expression and discussion that the good takes form by adjustment of private views to facts and needs brought to bear by criticism...... The full judgement of individuals based on the publicity of political discussion is ' public opinion.' In public opinion we have an existent contradiction. As public it is sound and true and contains the ethical spirit of the State. As expressed by individuals in their particular judgements, on which they plume themselves, it is full of falsehood and vanity........ If we restrict ourselves to the express utterance, we cannot possibly tell what the *public* is in earnest with...... because it does not know. . . .

But when the real will, the substantial reality, as the true inwardness of the public, is successfully divined and asserted, public opinion will always come round to it. . . . The man who can see and do what his age wills and demands is the great man of the age." [1]

The desirability that citizens should take part in public affairs lies in the necessity that they should have a concrete and therefore convinced sense of public needs and in the satisfaction of their impulse of self-assertion. " When they have contributed their opinions they are likely to acquiesce in what is done, to which each feels he has thrown in some element of suggestion and criticism." [2] " The people in a despotism pay light taxes, which in a constitutional State become larger through the people's own consciousness." [3]

In relation to other self-dependent States, the State has an independent sovereignty or exclusive individuality. This individuality is a primary freedom and the highest dignity of a people. For the preservation of this substantial, independent, and sovereign individuality of the State the citizens must sacrifice their property, life, and opinion if necessary. Herein lies the ethical element in war. [4] History teaches that successful wars have prevented civil broils and strengthened the internal power of the State. In peace the civil life becomes more and more extended. Each separate sphere walls itself in and becomes exclusive. In other words their particularity becomes more and more fixed and ossified And, at last, there is a stagnation of ethical and human development.

b. *International Law*

International law arises out of the relation of independent States to one another. The stipulations made between such States are provisional, but not eternally binding. But just as the individual person is not real unless related to others, so the State is not really individual unless related to other States. A State may not meddle with the internal

---

1. Hegel's view presented by Bosanquet in his Philos. Theory of State, pp. 285–7. See also K. Fischer, *op. cit.*, pp. 736, 737.
2. Cf. Hegel's Encyclopædia, section 544 and Bosanquet and K. Fischer, *ibid.*
3. Hegel's Phil. of Right, section 302.
4. Cf. before, pp. 10, 11 and K. Fischer, *op cit.*, p. 282.

affairs of another State ; yet it is essential for its completion that it should be recognized by others. But this recognition demands as a guarantee that it shall recognize those who recognize it, and maintain respect for their independence. Therefore they cannot be indifferent to its internal affairs.

c.   *Universal History*

" As the Spirit (*Geist*) of a special nation is actual and its liberty is under natural conditions, it admits on the nature-side the influence of geographical and climatic qualities. It is in time, and as regards its range and scope, has essentially a particular principle on the lines of which it must run through a development of its consciousness and its actuality. It has, in short, a history of its own. But as a restricted spirit its independence is something secondary ; it passes into universal history, the events of which exhibit the dialectic of the several spirits, — ' the judgement of the world.'

"This movement is the path of liberation for the spiritual substance, the deed by which the final aim of the world is realized in it, and the merely implicit spirit achieves consciousness and self-consciousness. It is thus the revelation and actuality of its essential and completed essence whereby it becomes to the outward eye a universal spirit — a world-mind. As this development is in time, and in real existence, as it is a history, its several stages and steps are the several national minds or spirits, each of which, as single and endued by nature with a specific character, is appointed to occupy only one grade and accomplish one task in the whole deed. . . .

" This liberation of mind as spirit in which it proceeds to come to itself and to realize the truth, — is the supreme right, the absolute law. The self-consciousness of a particular nation is a vehicle for the contemporary development of the universal Spirit in its actual existence ; it is the objective actuality in which that spirit for the time being invests its will. Against this absolute will the other particular national minds have no rights; that nation dominates the world ; but yet the universal will steps onward over its property for the time being, as over a special grade, and then delivers it over to its chance and doom.

" . . . The spirit which thinks in universal history, stripping off at the same time those limitations of the several national minds or spirits and its own temporal restrictions, lays hold of its concrete universality and rises to apprehend the absolute mind, as the eternally actual truth in which the contemplative reason enjoys freedom, while the necessity of nature and the necessity of history are only ministrant to its honor." [1]

The discussion of objective spirit leads to the realm of Absolute Spirit, which is the foundation of the ethical system. Ethical life is organic to the larger life of the human spirit, and this again organic to, and dependent on, the life and operation of the absolute and eternal spirit. Now Art, Religion, and Philosophy have this absolute and eternal spirit for their content. They differ in form, but the content for them is the same.

1. Hegel: Encyclopædia, sections 548–552.

CHAPTER VI

SOME CHARACTERISTICS AND DIFFICULTIES
IN HEGEL'S ETHICAL TEACHING

In the foregoing chapters Hegel's ethical teaching in his various works has been briefly presented according to the order of time in which they appeared. Now, before we go on to discuss anything further, it is perhaps worth while to throw a glance back upon them.

As has been mentioned, the "Treatise on Natural Right" and the "System of Ethicality" were written in the same year, 1802, and in the period when Hegel was still under the influence of Schelling. Hence the frequent appearance of such phrases as "potency," "identity," "indifference," etc., in the text of these two works. The positions presented and the method of treatment in these two works are for the most part identical. In addition to what has been pointed out in the respective chapters as to the minor differences between them and as to the slight advance made in the latter work, one more point is worth noticing here. It is that the "Treatise on Natural Right" is, except the last part, mainly an examination of the validity of the current views of group life and the legitimacy of the popular methods of treating such problems ; whereas the "System of Ethicality" is an analysis of the different modes of life themselves. And in the connecting system of the "System of Ethicality," Hegel has reached the notion of "Spirit" which is a prominent feature in his later philosophizing.

Next comes the "Phenomenology of Spirit" which marks the break of Hegel with Schelling, and so forms a distinctive point of departure in the development of Hegel's philosophical system. Originally it was designated as the first part of his "System der Wissenschaft" designed at that time.[1] His mode of approaching the problem of philosophy and the discussion which is here put forward are strikingly original, and the forms they assume are also novel. They are not only different from those of other philosophers, but even incongruous with those of his own other works. For instance, the sequence in which the various types or forms of Spirit appear, and the differentiation and classification of them are all at variance with the " Encyclopædia," the " Rechtsphilosophie," etc.

Ethically, this work has unique merits in its critical and appreciative exhibition of the various ethical views and theories possible, prevailing or once in vogue, such as Stoicism, Skepticism, Medieval Dualism, Moral Subjectivism, Sentimentalism, Mysticism, Asceticism, Rationalism, Romanticism, etc. It also surpasses his former works in furnishing abundant psychological discussions which are preliminary to ethics and in leading over into the realm of " Absolute Spirit " which transcends and underlies ethical experience. But the difficulty arising here is this: the views and theories of ethical life, the forms or types of Spirit, or the stages of the development of Spirit, set forth in the " Phenomenology " all have historical significance; but they are not presented in the same order as they manifested themselves in history. How does such discordance arise, if the real and the rational are identical? One may say, as K. Fischer[2] does, that the " Phenomenology of Spirit " is not the phenomena of Spirit. The characters which pass through the complex and confused, nay, at times, even wayward, process of life, do not know exactly what they are striving for. But the story-teller knows it well and can make the events happen in due order. Similarly, the phenomena of Spirit cannot help passing through a series of deceptions and self-deceptions which must be experienced and suffered in order to be known; the " Phenomenology of Spirit," on the other hand, sees through the deceptions and is free from them. Such an explanation is interesting, but does not face the question squarely.

1. See K. Fischer, *op. cit.*, p. 291 f.
2. See K. Fischer, *op. cit.*, p. 306.

Another possible method of explaining the difficulty is to insist that the "Phenomenology of Spirit" is not a Philosophy of History. What Hegel is seeking here is historical manifestations of the types or forms of Spirit to serve as illustrations of the stages of the self-development of Spirit. He finds the illustrations empirically; he analyzes them logically. So a stringent correspondence between the chronological sequence and logical sequence is not required. But as Professor J. Royce remarks, [1] " there are cases where the chronological relation itself becomes important." In such cases " the correspondence " between the evolution of humanity and the logical development of a science (i. e., a Phenomenology of Spirit) "seems to be more or less a guiding principle with Hegel," and "Hegel himself is likely to inform us explicitly that this is so." So the problem is really difficult to solve.

As a link between Hegel's "Voyage of Discovery" and his mature system, the "Philosophical Propaedeutic" may be mentioned. Here Hegel's theory of will appeared in a definite shape for the first time. His analysis of duties is also instructive. But, after all, these lecture-notes were meant only to teach the gymnasium pupils.

As has been said, [2] the "Encyclopædia" is the mature, authentic and complete statement of Hegel's philosophical system. As a statement of ethical doctrine the third part of it, i. e., the "Philosophy of Spirit," claims careful consideration. And of this again, the second division, i. e., the division on "Objective Spirit," is especially to be scrutinized. This division was elaborated by the philosopher himself into a "Philosophy of Right." But it would be unintelligible without some preliminary acquaintance with the leading facts of "Subjective Spirit." Hence the elaborate development of a theory of free will in the Introduction to the "Philosophy of Right." Since the Division on "Objective Spirit" and the "Philosophy of Right" are substantially the same, we have treated them in combination in the last chapter.

1. See Royce, Lecture on Modern Idealism, pp. 162–164.
2. See before p. 45

In comparison with Hegel's other ethical writings treated above, the "Philosophy of Spirit" and the "Philosophy of Right" are in their form and proceeding more similar to the early "Treatise on Natural Right" and the "System of Ethicality" than to the "Phenomenology of Spirit." The reason is that the "Phenomenology of Spirit" is meant to be an analysis of the actual phases of spiritual life, or the types or forms of Spirit, or if you like, of the stages of the evolution of Spirit, whereas the "Philosophy of Spirit," the "Philosophy of Right," and even the "Treatise on Natural Right" and the "System of Ethicality" are meant to consider the articulation of the principles of Spirit. The problem here is not their definite embodiment as phenomenal attitudes, but their interrelation as categories of the spiritual world. The one is more or less historical, while the other is logical.

In his "Treatise on Natural Right" and the "System of Ethicality" Hegel has not fully mastered the details of his task. During his "voyage of discovery" he was struggling hard to make his own way, but was not at all at ease. He reached in the main his final position by this work, but minor revisions were still requisite. For instance, the division of the categories of Spirit afterwards received some modification, and the æsthetic moment of Spirit had no place at all there. It is only in the "Encyclopædia" that Hegel first reached home, and there we can see him as a whole.

So much for review and comparison of the several works treated. Now, let us first of all point out that the most prominent feature throughout Hegel's ethical teaching is his unification of the ethical and moral with the actual. To him the task of political and moral philosophy is not the creation of a Utopia, as one might suppose; but an analysis of the existing system of rights, duties, and morals, so as to render them intelligible and somehow justifiable to reason. This is plainly set forth in his own preface to the "Philosophy of Right." "What is rational is real; and what is real is rational." So the aim of ethical writing is not to contrive any ideal society and moral order, but to comprehend and interpret existing reality, namely, to note the phases of rationality in existing forms and thus to endeavor to adjust men to reality. It is only an unfounded abstraction which can afford to set up a barrier between reason as self-conscious Spirit and reason as objectified reality. Such an abstraction deprives the Spirit of its satisfaction in reality, and so makes it poorer.

Hegel's unification or identification of the rational with the real, the ideal with the actual, is not haphazard or made without sufficient reason. Theoretically it is founded on his metaphysical position. In metaphysics he holds that reality is not distinct from ideality so far as reality means that something behaves conformably to its essential characteristics; or that something agrees with its notion. For example, in the expressions, 'a real man,' 'a real work of art,' what we mean by 'real' here is something true to its notion. On the other hand, ideality is not something outside of and beside reality; the notion of ideality lies just in its being the truth of reality. When reality is explicitly expressed as what it implicitly is, or promises to be, it is at once seen to be ideality.[1] With such a metaphysical principle in his mind, it is quite natural that he should not allow any separation of the ethical or moral from the actual; for what is true of the universe as a whole is more true of the preponderatingly spiritual elements therein — that is to say, more true of ethical life.

The other reason which prompted Hegel to posit this unification or identification is the influence he received from Hellenism. As we have seen in the foregoing chapters Hegel was greatly inspired by Hellenic civilization; and in his philosophizing he never forgets to refer and appeal from time to time to Hellenic antiquity. Now, Hellenic culture is preëminently characterized by an æsthetic view which sees the beautiful and ideal in the real. For the Greeks Nature is generally regarded as charming and valuable but seldom as hostile and evil. And in actual living, the free and glorious commonwealth of antiquity afforded the citizens so intensive a life that any sharp discrimination between the individual will and the universal purpose had not arisen. Nor had any dissatisfaction with existing reality come to be felt. This

1. See Encyclopædia, sect. 91.

made upon Hegel a deep impression and contributed much to the formation of his system.

Still another reason perhaps was the historical situation in Europe at that moment. Germany was for a while crushed by Napoleon. The War of Liberation succeeded merely in shaking off the French yoke. National unity, strength, and wisdom were still lacking to Germany. But vague aspirations after a freer life, accompanied by rhetorical enthusiasm and momentary emotion, are, to Hegel, good for nothing. According to his convictions, the German nation could be saved only by the formation of a strong, united and wisely governed state. That is, the ideal, the spiritual freedom of the nation, could not be accomplished save through the instrumentality of the real, the institutional life developed here and now.

Hegel in his unification or identification of the real with the rational, or the ideal with the actual, is accused of taking the existing régime as final. [1] Such acceptance or " worship " of " Actualism " has been deemed fatal to moral progress. But it is quite plain from Hegel's own language that he never posits or implies moral stagnation. On the contrary his " Philosophy of Spirit " [2] and " Philosophy of Right " make it very clear that the institutional life of any particular nation or age is limited by geographical and temporary conditions. Being finite and limited, it must needs be subject to the process of Dialectic — the Dialectic between the spirits of the several nations and ages. In this Dialectic process each nation or age can and indeed must make contributions through mutual mediation to the furtherance of morality and ethical life as well as to the increase of the common stock of human culture in general; but none can hope alone to attain perfection and finality. Even in his early days Hegel had already stated this point emphatically. [3] Indeed he insists that the ideal can be achieved only through the real, but this is quite different from " worshiping the existing reality." Again, he refuses to take moral progress as the task

1. For example, A. Seth in his " Hegelianism and Personality."
2. See sections on Universal History.
3. See before p. 13.

of philosophy. But this is due to, and consistent with, his view that the function of philosophy is explanation, not creation. And to exclude one thing from the task of a certain science is quite different from denying the reality or existence of the same. The foregoing accusation cannot, therefore, be fairly brought against Hegel.

Hegel in this unification or identification of the real with the rational or ideal is also accused of having overlooked or neglected the fact that there are many things irrational and unsatisfactory or even positively bad in the existing world. But his conception of the real as something which is true to its notion and not merely appearing or possessing real (as opposed to imaginary) existence only in passing phenomena, blunts the edge of such criticism. Things vary in degree of truth or in their adequacy to their respective notions. Hence there arise degrees of reality, or rather of adequacy to notion. Only the truly real is thoroughly rational. Reality is rational with reference to a whole. Implications and indications of rationality are present everywhere, in the form and intelligibility of nature as well as in human thought, conduct, relations, institutions, and creations. But this does not mean that all the variously differentiated details of reality are equally rational. Such a qualification has been regarded as renouncing the claim to an absolute system. However, Hegelianism is, or can be, an absolute system only in the sense that it exhibits at once the constituting or organizing and governing principles of Reality (the task of Metaphysics) and the categories of the process of its manifestation (the task of Logic). It is absolute in so far as it exhausts the principle and the framework of the process of experience. We cannot get behind a unity of the principle with its process. But it is not absolute in the sense that all the detailed phenomenal appearances or even illusions happening in connection with its manifestation, are comprehended in a single synthesis. What we may charge upon Hegel in this connection is perhaps that his proposal for a pure interpretation of existing reality without construction of any kind, is a program incapable of being carried out. The emphasis upon this thing or neglect of that, the criticism of one thing or appreciation of another, cannot help assuming and betraying some principle of judgment. Such unconsciously assumed principles determine tacitly for the thinker what is essential, and so, desirable or ideal.

The subject matter of ethics is, of course, the intelligent moral life which is the manifestation of Spirit in the objective world. The precise starting point with Hegel, however, is Will, which is the volitional functioning of Spirit. In his earlier writings this is not so exactly formulated. For in the "System of Ethicality," the phrase "desire," in the "Phenomenology," the phrase "moral consciousness," were employed; whereas in the "Encyclopædia" and the "Philosophy of Right" in the corresponding passages he uses the term "will." But what Hegel has in mind is the same thing.

Will, with Hegel,[1] is not to be taken as a faculty diverse from intelligence. On the contrary, it is but another form of intelligence. To be more accurate, genuine will is intelligence translating itself into determinate being. It is cognition completed and passing into actualization. True will, however, is quite different from desire and impulse, which are blind tendencies to activity, not yet mediated by reason. Desire and impulse are given conditions common to all animals, while real will is a faculty formed through the discipline of human culture. Will is the consummation, the ideal consummation, of a process by which the subject or moral agent raises himself out of his absorption in sensation, desire, and impulse; thus establishing within himself an ideal realm, an organization of ideas and ideals, a self-consciousness and a self.

Intelligent will is essentially free. Freedom is the very substance and characteristic of will. Stripped of freedom, will has no significance. It brings forth a spiritual world on earth only by virtue of its freedom. Only, it should be remembered that such a freedom is a freedom acquired or earned. It is the result of the self-realization of Spirit; but not a given fact of consciousness.

Freedom is, of course, opposite to external determination or mere submission to authority. But freedom of a genuine will, as Hegel

---

1. See the "Philosophy of Right": Introduction.

teaches, is quite different from (1) license.   Understanding **freedom in the sense** of license, we say that a man is free only when he may do whatever he chooses and however he pleases.   Such freedom, i. e., license, is not compatible with any mediation through reason, nor with any respect to social and ethical order.   Real freedom is also different from (2) arbitrariness.   When a man acts in an arbitrary spirit he does certain things in a certain way steadfastly, but without giving any reason, or upon grounds which are merely one-sided, abstract and dogmatic. Freedom is, again, different from (3) caprice.   In the state of caprice, one does things without deliberate consideration.   For instance, a man at one time chooses to promote a certain social and ethical institution ; then he comes to the conclusion that the same institution ought to be destroyed.   To-day a woman marries a man with great joy and enthusiasm ; to-morrow she finds that she must divorce him.   Such action is determined by casual conceit or pure whim, or by momentary inclination and likeness.   Genuine freedom is, once more, different from (4) option or the formal freedom of undeveloped will.   Taking freedom in this spirit, a man deems himself free when he finds that he may choose to do something just as well as not at all ; or to do this just as well as that ; or to act in one way just as well as in another.   Such freedom is nothing but indeterminateness.

Freedom of the above-named sorts is irrational and inconsistent ; for in no case is it mediated through all-round consideration and determined by well-adopted principles.   Such freedom is really no freedom except in form.   It is controlled or dictated by natural desire and impulse or momentary conjunctures, and, consequently, is dependent upon outward circumstances, not upon the will itself.   Decisions made by such freedom will always be haunted by the regret or the fancy that it would have been better if one had been pleased to decide in favor of the reverse course.   It is, therefore, self-contradictory and must involve the whole mass of desires, whims, inclinations, and dogmatic fancies in a common destruction.   The reason is not that natural men, or undeveloped wills or irreflective and inconsiderate souls, will one thing at the expense of everything else, but simply that they do not begin to deliberate upon the bearing and implication of action, and so really do not know what they are doing.

True freedom of the real will is, on the other hand, at once free and determined. It is incompatible with predetermination and coercion by a foreign power, but nevertheless firmly determinate and self-consistent. In other words, it is determined by the intelligent, self-characterized will to realize itself. But as soon as realization begins, certain steps must needs be taken. So in a certain sense, it may be said that true freedom is self-willed necessity. It should be remembered, however, that such self-determination is not a determination by the abstract self, for the will here is fully developed and mediated through all-round reason. To be more accurate, true freedom, in the spirit of Hegel's teaching, can be accomplished only after the genuine will, as reasoned and intelligent, has formed a definite view or theory of life through a dialectic mediation with the facts of the natural, social, and aspirational worlds, and at the same time through a redintegration and systematization of its own manifoldly differentiated and diametrically conflicting purposes and postulates of life. Such view or theory of life gives rise to, nay, determines, a scheme of conduct or a system of the various modes of life. In such a scheme of conduct, or system of the various modes of life, each purpose, desire, inclination or other motive to action finds its proper place and the appropriate effort necessary for its satisfaction. But with this view or theory of a determinate type of life the will has identified itself ; hence it wills nothing but what is justified by the agent's view or theory of life, and falls within the scheme of conduct or the system of the various modes of life thereby determined. The will is, therefore, always at home with itself ; conscious of itself as a whole, and of the fact that its content is intrinsically firm and fast, and at the same time its own. No doubt it conforms to the current morals, laws, customs, traditions, and manners of corporate humanity ; but in so doing it has recognized these as virtually its own. As it has appropriated and accepted them for itself anew, they become thereby "inwardized." In this sense, free will is infinite and absolute. It wills what it is. It is its own object — never confronted by any limitation external to it.

Hegel's doctrine of the moral agent or moral will is, indeed, thoroughly intellectualistic. With him the moral will is strictly guided by intelligence, and is motivated little, if at all, by emotion. This has been seen already in the preceding paragraphs; but in the first part of the " Philosophy of Spirit " and in his preface to the " Philosophy of Right ".it is still more plainly set forth. `

From the preface to the "Philosophy of Right" it may be learned that the truths with regard to ethical life, ethical principles, ethical ideals, and to the actual world of right, the state, the government. and the constitution, cannot proceed from each man's heart, feeling, and enthusiasm. They must be apprehended in intelligence and by intelligence ; they must be given definite, general and rational form. But feeling, which seeks its own pleasure, and conscience which finds Right in private conviction, are liable to be contingent, random, and fanciful. It is a self-assertion of the honor of man to approve of nothing in sentiment which is not justified by intelligence.

In his "Philosophy of Spirit," intellectualism appears strikingly also in connection with the idea of the freedom of will. He says, "True liberty in the shape of moral life, consists in the will finding its purpose in a universal content. . . . But such a content is only possible in thought and through thought." [1]   An appeal to the sense (or feeling) of right and morality, as well as of religion, to man's benevolent disposition, to his heart generally, or to the subject so far as the various practical feelings are all combined in it . . . has oftentimes, and perhaps rightly, been regarded as indispensable to keep moral life and religion alive. But according to Hegel, such an appeal has legitimate meaning only " so far as it implies (1) that these ideas are immanent in man's own life, and (2) that when feeling is opposed to the logical understanding, it, and not the partial abstractions of the latter, may be the totality." [2]   And even then, Hegel holds, the superiority of intelligence is still to be maintained. For "feeling too may be one-sided, unessential and bad. The rational,

1. Sect. 469.
2. Sect. 471.

which exists in the shape of rationality when it is apprehended by thought, is the same content as the good practical feeling has, but presented in its universality and necessity, in its objectivity and truth." [1]

In the same connection Hegel then proceeds to insist strongly upon the superiority and necessity of intelligence and the unreliability and negligibility of feeling and the heart. He says, " It is on the one hand silly to suppose that in the passage from feeling to law and duty (i. e., *to the realm of intelligence*) there is any loss of import and excellence ; it is this passage which lets feeling first reach its truth. It is equally silly to consider intellect as superfluous or even harmful to feeling, heart, and will; the truth or the actual rationality of the heart and will can only be at home in the universality of intellect, and not in the singleness of feeling as feeling. If feelings are of the right sort, it is because of their quality or contents, which is right only so far as it is intrinsically universal or has its source in the thinking mind. . . . " On the other hand, it is pernicious or even worse to cling to feeling and heart in place of the intelligent rationality of law, right and duty ; because all that the former holds more than the latter is only the particular subjectivity with its vanity and caprice. For the same reason it is out of place in a scientific treatment of feelings to deal with anything beyond their form, and to discuss their content ; for the latter, when thought, is precisely what constitutes, in their universality and necessity, the rights and duties which are the true works of mental autonomy. So long as we study practical feelings and dispositions specially we have only to deal with the selfish, bad and evil; it is these alone which belong to the individuality which retains its opposition to the universal; their content is the reverse of rights and duties, and precisely in that way do they — but only in antithesis to the latter — retain a specialty of their own." [2]

This thoroughgoing intellectualism in Hegel is again due to the influence of Greek philosophy. From the time when Socrates taught that " Virtue is Knowledge," Greek Ethics showed a distinct bias

---

1. Sect. 471.
2. Philosophy of Spirit, sec. 471. Italics mine.

towards intellectualism, although Plato and Aristotle endeavored to moderate it to some extent. Hegel was so deeply inspired by Greek culture that he could by no means free himself from its prejudices.

Another cause which may have prompted him to such a position was his intention to correct the faults of the Romantic movement; which, as we know, was dominated by indulgence of imagination, caprice, and waywardness. One example from Hegel's own personal experience may suffice to illustrate what is meant here : Schelling, A. Schlegel, and his wife, Caroline, the most distinguished representatives of the so-called younger Romanticism, were all close friends at Jena ; Schlegel and his wife Caroline had so far been a harmonious couple. But after Schlegel went to Berlin, the idol of the Romanticists' circle, Caroline, married Schelling. Yet they all three kept on good terms with one another till her death. Hegel was impatient of such extravagant sentimentalism. His attempt to chasten overindulgence in emotion may have led him to another extreme. In other words, he might have tolerated some emotional element in his ethical teaching if it were not that the Romanticists had insisted upon, or rather overemphasized it almost to the exclusion of intelligence and deliberate volition.

As an attempt to correct the sentimentalism of the Romanticists, Hegel's work may be said to be successful. And so far we can sympathize with its success. But, as a constructive system, such an ethics of pan-intellectualism has, like the Greek culture, its points of weakness. The main difficulty is that human reason is a single whole ; its emotional, volitional, and thinking elements are distinct functions, but not separate faculties. As they form only one reason, when one is called in to play its part, the others are also at work. They never become entirely inert. Therefore, the function of thinking cannot in our experience be entirely independent of, or freed from, the influence of feeling and will, or emotion and the unmediated forms of will, desire and impulse, although it may be regarded as higher than the latter. Emotion is transient and unstable, while reason is tranquil and enduring. But, sometimes, the momentary force of emotion proves irresistible. As Spinoza says, " Desire arising from a true knowledge of good and evil can be destroyed or checked by many other desires arising from emotions by which we are assailed." [1]   In reply to this Hegel may say, as Socrates substantially did, if your knowledge of the good and evil surrenders to your emotions, you cannot be said to have a true knowledge of them.   But Spinoza says further, " A true knowledge of good and evil cannot check any emotion by virtue of its being true, but only in so far as it is considered as an emotion." [2]   Again, " An emotion can only be controlled or destroyed by another emotion contrary thereto and with more power for controlling emotion." [3]   The reason, Spinoza maintains,[4] must be transformed into an emotion or impulse of " self-preservation " which is the psychological root of morality or basis of virtue.   Personally I admit that Spinoza may have overstated the case.   But what he says in this regard certainly possesses some truth.   It may be seen in our experience that mere abstract notion and theoretical insight are impotent.   Deliberate volition and action which has moral value can be attained only when the reason is allied to and aided by emotion, and supported, nay, obeyed, by desire and impulse.   But in order to secure and make use of the assistance of emotion and the obedience of desire and impulse, reason must needs pay them due respect and give them appropriate satisfaction.   Indeed, being lower in character, they must be purified and transformed through the mediation of reason.   But, nevertheless, they are essential elements ; reason cannot do away with them; and they must in some way, preferably, of course, in a reasoned way, be satisfied, otherwise there can be no harmony or inner justice.

Hegel himself has unconsciously felt the need of this.   In insisting upon the performance of duty he alleges as its recompense, besides the protection of person and property, the inner satisfaction of the individual's real self and the personal consciousness and self-respect which comes from a membership of the whole.[5]   This is little different

---

1. Spinoza, Ethics, Book IV, Prop. 15.
2. Spinoza, *op. cit.*, Book IV, Prop. 14.
3. Spinoza, *op. cit.*, Book IV, Prop. 7.
4. *Ibid.*, Book III, Props. 7–9.
5. See Philosophy of Right, sect. 261.

from an appeal to the motivating power of emotion. And he has also recognized that political disposition or patriotism in general is confidence or *faith* in the State, a condition which consists in emotion rather than in knowledge; though it may attain to more or less intelligent insight.[1] And in allowing the citizens to participate in legislation, the main purpose which he has in view is to enable them to enjoy the satisfaction of feeling themselves to count for something.[2] And his acknowledgment of the force of a sense of " Fatherland " in the state of war,[3] when elaborated, cannot be held to be different from the tone of Fichte's famous addresses to the German nation, namely, a mere appeal to patriotic sentiment. In anothr connection in the " Philosophy of Right," he says, " In the state, we do not find love; there one is conscious of the unity as the unity of law, there the content must be rational and I must know it."[4] It is true that the content must be rational and we must know it. But we nevertheless still need a love of country and a sense of the necessity and pride of being able to maintain its dignity, honor and glory; otherwise there can be no earnest service to support the union. Such a Love is, in Spinoza's language, an intellectual love.

As has been repeatedly said in the foregoing paragraphs, the will, intelligent will, or rather the volitional functioning of Objective Spirit, is self-determinate. This means that it chooses for itself a certain type of life, and takes definite steps to realize the same. This certain type of life consists of, nay, is substantiated, in the several forms or modes in which the will or the volitional functioning of Objective Spirit in general determines itself and manifests itself. Now, these forms or modes are what our philosopher terms " rights." [5] They are to be formulated into a system of positive laws, while the intelligent free will

1. See Philosophy of Right, sect. 268.
2. See Encycl., sect. 544 and Philos. of Right, sections 315 – 318.
3. See Encycl., sect. 546.
4. Sect. 158.
5. See note at end of this chapter.

remains the indwelling spirit of them. The relation of free will to Right is, therefore, as K. Fischer says,[1] "Like that of soul to body."

Right as defined above may be taken in a comprehensive sense as including not merely juristic right, but all the forms or modes of the whole process of the manifestation of intelligent will in the actual world. As Hegel tells us, " a mode of existence is a right," [2] " by the word Right we signify not only civil right, which is its usual meaning, but also morality, ethicality, and world-history " ; [3] or as he expresses it otherwise, right is "the actual body of all the conditions of freedom " ; [4] "the System of Right is the realm of realized freedom, the world of Spirit produced out of itself as a second nature." [5]

As has been seen in the preceding chapters, especially the last one, Right is distinguished by our philosopher as (1) the abstract right of the abstract person, or "unmediated" will to property in the realm of Law; (2) the reflective right of the " self-conscious " subject or reflective will, to Morality based upon conscience ; (3) the concrete right of the ethical group, or the " mediated " and " substantial " will, to Ethicality determined by "General Will " and obtained through common living together; and this is differentiated further into (a) the right of the family ; (b) the right of the community; (c) the right of the nation ; and (d) the right of humanity. These " rights " being finite and limited, are oftentimes found in collision and contradiction. Thus they are unstable and cannot rest within themselves. That is, they must needs fall into the process of " Dialectic."

Now, " Dialectic " is a fundamental metaphysical doctrine in the Hegelian philosophy and is universally applied in Hegel's writings. The soundness of such application in general and the greater precautions he should have taken will be discussed later. Here we may content ourselves with a bare statement of the doctrine and a glimpse of its application to our problem in hand.

1. *Op. cit.*, p. 690.
2. Encyclopædia, sect. 486.
3. Philosophy of Right, sect. 83 note.
4. Encyclopædia, sect. 486.
5. Philosophy of Right, sect. 4.

"Dialectic," Hegel tells us,[1] is the very nature and essence of everything predicated by the finite categories—the law of things and of the finite as a whole. Wherever there is life, wherever there is movement, wherever *anything* is *carried* into *effect* in the actual world, there "Dialectic" is at work. It is obviously seen in general experience that everything finite, instead of being stable and ultimate, is rather changeable and transient; and this illustrates exactly what is meant by that "Dialectic" whereby the finite as implicitly other than what it is, is forced beyond its own immediate or implicit being to turn into its opposite. "Dialectic," in other words, is the indwelling tendency outwards by which the one-sidedness and limitations of the finite are seen in their true light and shown to be the negation of themselves. However, it should be understood, the limitations do not come from without; the very nature of the finite is the cause of its own abrogation : it passes into its counterpart also by its own act.

Applying this metaphysical principle to the ethico-social world, Hegel treats the development of free will or the manifestation of Objective Spirit in its various forms of " right " as a process of "Dialectic." His ethical writings, especially the "Philosophy of Spirit" and the "Philosophy of Right," seek, and take much pains, to trace this process. The whole course of the immanent "Dialectic," as is shown by Hegel, runs as the Objective Spirit moves through the various forms of its self-manifestation or, as the free will assumes successively the several " rights." In other words, it proceeds from the most abstract and undeveloped to the most concrete and ripest. To be more specific still, the most abstract right is that of the abstract person to property. As all abstract persons have the same right, some conflicts are bound to arise. Hence the necessity of an adjustment by laws. The power of law, however, cannot be arbitrarily imposed from without upon the subject. It must be the direct expression of the nature of the subject, or self-consciously appropriated by it. This is the reflective right of the self-conscious subject to the morality of conscience. But subjective

---

1. See Encyclopædia, sect. 81.

conscience is liable to be mere caprice. It thus gives way to the right of the socialized group or of the collective spirit or general will of a nation to ethicality. The immediate form of ethicality is found in the family, which has the right to an independent existence and unimpeded prosperity. But the family cannot be extended on any large scale; it naturally passes over into the realm of civic community where the particular "*Stände*" and corporations find their rights as distinct from private interests. Now, particular "*Stände*" or corporations have their being only on condition of the existence of a larger organization—the national state—which alone can command and uphold a relatively independent, free expression of a certain type of life willed by the nation itself. This is the right of nationality. Nations, however, are limited by both spatial and temporal conditions. National culture, therefore, cannot escape the judgment of universal history whereby it is transcended. This gives rise to the right of humanity to a rational continuous development of universal Spirit. This, however, is still not the final stage. It, by implication and indication points to, and leads over into, the realm of Absolute Spirit, into the higher forms of the Spirit in the spheres of Art, Religion, and Philosophy.

Note to the term "Recht." This term in the Hegelian philosophy has puzzled many students. Some regard it as incapable of being translated into English, while others have rendered it by the terms "Right" or "Law," which are, of course, inadequate. As is expounded in the foregoing pages, it is quite intelligible. But, all the same, I think it furnishes an example of the confusion of terminology in Hegel. In his Logic, the first main Division is designated as the "Doctrine of Being"; the second, "Doctrine of Essence"; the third, "Doctrine of Notion." But "Being," "Essence," and "Notion" are only the first particular categories under the respective main Divisions. Under the same main Divisions there are categories—say, "Becoming," "Measure," "Actuality," "Idea," which are more adequate and complete than the very categories—i. e., "Being," "Essence," and "Notion," which Hegel employed to designate the whole Divisions, and consequently, the former cannot be covered by the latter. In other words, Hegel's denotation is incapable of connoting the content assigned to it. Now, what is true of the Logic can also be held true of the "Philosophy of Right." "Right" is only the first particular category, under the Division of "Objective Spirit." It is too narrow and so is inadequate to designate the whole Division; for under the same Division there are categories, i. e., "Morality" and "Ethicality," which are more adequate and complete than "Right." Of course, Hegel has a right to use words in a certain sense which is unique to him. Therefore, he may call "Morality" "Ethicality," and Universal History certain forms of "Right." But there is no reason why he should not have called them something else, so that the name might. as it should, convey what is meant. Such confusion of terminology as we find in Hegel is not a little misleading.

CHAPTER VII

OBJECTIVE MANIFESTATION AND OBJECTIVE NORM

IN HEGEL'S ETHICS

Because of Hegel's unification or identification of the real with the rational, or the ideal with the actual, his ethical writings have been complicated with abundant discussions about economical, political, social, and juristic problems. Possession, property, contract, purpose and responsibility, intention and welfare, all have relation to the natural world, while Ethicality deals directly with one or another form of society. The students of Hegel at this point have oftentimes complained that his ethical writings are not ethical or moral enough. They are indiscriminately mixed up with economics, sociology, political science, jurisprudence, and history; and they contain too much of these studies, and too little of Ethics or Moral Philosophy proper.

As an answer to such criticism, we may first of all quote Wallace: " In philosophy at least," he says, [1] " it is difficult or rather impossible to draw a hard and fast line which shall demarcate ethical from non-ethical characters. . . . Kant, as we know, attempted to do so, but with the result that he was forced to add a doubt whether a purely moral act could ever be said to exist; or rather to express the certainty that if it did, it was forever inaccessible to observation."

Without indulging in polemics, let us conscientiously inquire into the real justifiability of the inclusion of the natural and social in the ethical and moral. Man is a real and concrete being. He is born and lives in certain natural and social situations from which he can never be abstracted or separated. If he is to be understood in his entirety, he

---

1. Introd., Essays to Hegel's Phil. of Mind, p. 118.

must be explained in connection with all of these. True it is that he is essentially also a moral and spiritual character. But his morality and spirituality in the truer sense cannot remain a mere state of mind, but must be expressed in activities of the natural and social world functioning towards the realization of spiritual freedom; that is, must pass through the medium of the natural and the social.

The natural is not, as is often supposed, inimical to, but is, on the contrary, capable of mediation with the moral and spiritual. In lending itself to the appropriation and transformation of human activities and thus helping to relieve the " tension " between human needs and their satisfaction, nature already serves moral purposes. And as a medium for the expression of æsthetic feeling and contemplation, nature has attained to a realm which Hegel calls " Absolute Spirit." Not to go too far afield, let us recall the old teaching of Aristotle; to be a good man, one must have sufficient goods. And, as elementary modes and forms in which the will realizes its freedom, formative labor, occupancy, possession, property, etc., which have direct concern with nature, all have moral values. Hence they are indispensable, no matter how crude may be their modes and forms.

Through the institution of contract, man's relation to nature passes over into that between men. Only in so far as human relations are properly formed and further and further developed, are the higher ends of Man capable of realization; for, as we know, literature, science, art, religion, moral life, etc., cannot be achieved save by the coöperation and through the mediation of social groups. Indeed, the regulation and adjustment of economic, political, and juristic institutions are the subordinate means to the realization of spiritual freedom as the primary end. But, so long as they are and remain the necessary means by which alone the higher ends are achieved, no ethical system can be said to be complete without having dealt with their governing principles, seeing that they form an essential factor in the end itself. And these principles, on the other hand, are so closely connected with ethical and philosophical principles properly so-called that they can never be separated from the latter without losing their significance and intelligibility.   These principles, therefore, will continue to belong to the sphere of Ethics and Philosophy, while minute details of purely economic, political, and juristic character may be relegated to special branches of study.

Indeed, an ethical treatise cannot help including some discussions of the fundamental principles of economic, social, political, and juristic studies; for ethical and moral life, as we have just shown, can be realized only in and through the objective, the natural and social world.   However, it is also natural and inevitable that the expressions of the ethical and moral spirit as such in the objective, the natural and social, world are usually found inadequate to its notion; for cases of imperfection and contradiction, not to say evil, are abundant everywhere.   This inadequacy leads to dissatisfaction with the world of existing reality.   And, when to this dissatisfaction are added the momentary effects of pessimistic thoughts, the hope of living a beautiful, good and rational life in the actual world has sometimes been deliberately given up.   Thus the agent flees from the inflictions and limitations of incompleteness and particularity; and attempts to attain complete moral and ethical life otherwise than through activities in the objective world.   Such an attempt, when persisted in, simply results in either pure mentalism (or subjectivism), or extravagant mysticism.

By pure mentalism or subjectivism I mean something like what Hegel describes in his "Phenomenology of Spirit" under the heading of the "beautiful soul";[1] the phrase extravagant mysticism, I suppose, needs no explanation.   Both pure mentalism or subjectivism and extravagant mysticism have one common characteristic, that is, they try to escape from contact with actuality, so as to be able to get rid of the inflictions of contradiction, limitation, imperfection, etc., which will otherwise disfigure and stain the purity and splendour of the inner being.   But there is also a sharp difference between them, that is, pure mentalism or subjectivism seeks to supplement this negative flight by a recoil to the inner world of "Subjective Spirit," while extravagant

1. See before pp. 39–41.

mysticism seeks the same end by attempting to soar up into the world of "Absolute Spirit." Both pure mentalism or subjectivism and extravagant mysticism are very alluring and fascinating, especially to the Oriental mind. Since they have, from time to time, seduced many so-called higher souls and rigorous moralists, it is necessary to examine them a little closely here.

As we have just mentioned, pure mentalism or subjectivism is something like what Hegel in his "Phenomenology of Spirit" describes under the heading of the "beautiful soul." Besides what has been said in that connection, we may add that pure mentalism or subjectivism holds to the idea that after the flight from contact with the objective and actual world, the subject may return to the subjective world, and man abide within this isolated pure mentality or subjectivity as in a sanctuary, where morality may be pursued with a clear conscience and certainty of conviction but independently of outward approbation and obligation with its consequent perplexity and incompleteness. Here the virtues which the agent aspires to achieve are self-control, subjugation of the flesh and its lusts, suppression of impulse and desire, endurance of hardship, indifference to distress, inward harmony, ease and simplicity of mental tone, gracefulness of imagination, sweetness of temper, etc. If there is any activity at all beyond abstract, isolated subjectivity, it consists, as Hegel describes, only in the manifestation and expression of such states of consciousness, in communication and discourse about them with kindred souls, in mutual corroboration and assurance of the purity and conscientiousness of those souls, not in activity and deed in the objective world. It is believed that by such discipline internal peace, liberty, self-satisfaction, perfection, and holiness are to be attained.

Such a doctrine of the moral life is, from the standpoint of the Hegelian philosophy, fundamentally unsound. In the first place, the idea (*Vorstellung*) of pursuing a moral life in an isolated sanctuary of pure subjectivity is theoretically inconceivable. In human experience there can be no subject apart from an object. "The dualism between the object and subject — between man and his world — which the Stoic sought to escape by withdrawing into himself, follows him, as the Sceptic showed, even into the inner life. The soul opposed to the world and emptied of it is found to be opposed to, and emptied of, itself." [1] That is to say, the opposition between subjectivity and objectivity must be overcome by a reconciliation, but cannot be cancelled by eliminating the latter from the former. Any attempt to do away with the object would result in doing away with the subject itself, i.e., in suicide.

In practice the necessity of objectivity is still more obvious than in theory. As we know, the mere development of mental capacities, the formation of moral dispositions or the making of an ethical character, already presupposes an objective, a natural and social, world as its field of discipline and exercise. And in the ethical and moral life, so far as the category of realization and actuality goes, a man means only what he does.[2] "If his virtue, morality, etc., are only inwardly his — that is, if they exist only in his intentions and sentiments, and are not identified with or realized in outward acts, the one-half of him is just as hollow and empty as the other." [3]

In other words, the attitude of mere subjectivity or pure mentality is untenable. It must come to terms with objectivity and find satisfaction in it. Mere subjectivity or mentality means " negation." [4] A contemplated end, i.e., the hope of living a certain type of life, amounts merely to an expression of "want," if left unrealized. A state of "negation" and "want" is a state of unrest, is certain to issue in revolt, is no freedom, no peace. Freedom and peace can be restored only by "negating this negation," or satisfying the "want," i.e., by realizing the contemplated end in the objective world; but not by fleeing from contact with the latter and suppressing or renouncing the former. To dispose of an end merely by suppressing or renouncing the pursuit of it is a self-deception, for the desire for the contemplated end is not thereby satisfied—except in a momentary and simulated way—and the inner contradiction of " tension " and " want " will sooner or later come

1. E. Caird: Hegel, pp. 207-208, extracted from Hegel's Phenomenology of Spirit.
2. See Hegel: Phil. of Right, sect. 124.
3. Hegel: Logic, sect. 140.
4. See *ibid.*, sections 204 – 206.

to be felt again.   To get rid of this inner contradiction by disregarding it is a mistaken theory; it is impracticable so long as the subject is not reduced to an empty, abstract, indifferently pure being.   If the subject were reduced to this condition, it would contradict his purpose; for such a pure being is insignificant, poor and hollow, rather than such a perfect and holy being as the moral agent under this mistaken theory aims at becoming.

Why then should one pursue such an indifferent empty life?   The agent by such barren self-assertion could find no inner wealth to console himself.   The "consciousness of the loss of all reality in the assurance of the self" [1] will, as soon as Scepticism sets in, be followed by the "consciousness of the loss of the last assurance," [1] because "the self so asserted is rather absolutely estranged from itself." [1]   Like the Stoic consciousness of the absolute worth and dignity of the rational life which is present to each individual, such a theory of moral life, when taken earnestly and matured in a "deeper realization of its own meaning," [2] will soon "pass into an abject self-despair, into a sense of infinite want, into a *hypnotized* readiness to accept *anything* outward which may deliver it from its own inward emptiness." [2]   The only alternative to this is to give up life, both inner and outer alike.   Indeed, the despairing agent, if he does not turn to accept any objectivity which is ready at hand for his world, is destined to fade away.   One example quoted by Hegel [3] is that of Cato, who, after the downfall of the Roman republic, could live no longer.   He had no will to live because he could find no end to serve.   What he regarded as alone valuable had been lost and could not possibly be recovered.

Extravagant mysticism, on the other hand, attempts to supplement the flight from contact with the actual world by a desperate leap.   The process of it begins with some subjective discipline in lofty feeling, saintly sentiment, and high-mindedness; also in introspective observation,

1.   See E. Caird: Hegel, pp. 205, 206.
2.   See E. Caird: *op. cit.*, p. 208.   Italics mine.
3.   See Phil. of Spirit, sect. 406.

fanatic imagination, picturesque thinking and luminous vision; and again, in faith, conviction, energizing and obedience; and finally, through some enthusiastic moments of ecstatic meditation and mystic contemplation, it passes directly over to the realm of Absolute Spirit where self-expansion, wholeness and holiness, nay, union with the Absolute, are supposed to be achieved.

Such a theory of moral life is no less unsound than that of pure mentalism or subjectivism, For the idea *(Vorstellung)* of a leap from the world of subjective spirit to the Absolute is fantastic. The world of Absolute Spirit is not a last refuge from the hard and bitter reality; nor can it be reached by the plunge of faith, which seems rather the leap of despair. It is not a world *par excellence* ' other ' than the present; one longed for, presaged, beheld in dreamy vision, but unperceived by the clear light of intelligence. It is not attained by shutting one's eyes to reality and flying on the wings of momentary mystic enthusiasm to the better land and to the presence of the divine, infinite, and Absolute ; but rather by persistence in unfolding, expanding, adjusting, recombining, transforming, and fortifying those partial glimpses of the divine and absolute which occur in every vision of the finite and relative. The Absolute Spirit is, in other words, the comprehensive totality which is a complete organism; it is the unity of notion and objectivity or knowledge and life which, left to themselves, are all finite and relative. This unity is called by Hegel the Idea. Idealism means " seeing all things in the Idea." The ' Idea ' is everywhere in nature although nowhere clearly, or as a whole: or what is the same thing, nature is essentially a world of reason and intelligence, though intelligence petrified and fragmentary. Man's place in the universe is to fulfil the promise and indication of nature to the full reality of spirit; to fulfil it by intelligent, purposeful, and well-adapted activities in economic, legal, political, and social relations, in the ethical and moral life, and, in a more universal measure, in Art, Religion, and Speculation. But, at any rate, he must live through the life of the actual world, while limitations and short-comings are in process of being transcended. He cannot leap out of the actual world. He is a child of nature and of society. He must rest on, and grow out of, a natural basis of existence, and draw spiritual nutriment from society. Nature is elastic and adaptable to spiritual purpose, It serves to make man's spirituality visible and actual. Society, on the other hand, is positively productive of spirituality. It furnishes the background, and helps to evoke the universal and rational, but is purged of the particular and capricious elements of the individual subjective spirit through the process of mediation.

Apart from the medium of nature and society, all efforts made to attain to the realm of Absolute Spirit are futile. Over-strained ascetic self-tormenting and mystic contemplation, after the agent has been physically exhausted, alike lead to pathological conditions, from which hallucination and other hysteric phenomena result. The agent under such abnormal conditions loses his ' common sense.' He is liable to fall into all sorts of ridiculous, vicious, and even sinful acts, while he may think he is acting as if he were already in the realm of Absolute Spirit. Such a discipline is no path to the realm of Absolute Spirit, but rather the path to an abyss of perdition.

The foregoing paragraphs have proved that the ethical and moral life can be achieved only through activities, i. e., through conduct in the objective world. Hence the justification of including discussions of nature and society in the ethical and moral sphere. Activities or conduct, however, in the objective world must be determined by some definite objective Norm. This Hegel found in the conceptions, dispositions, manners, disciplines, morals, customs, traditions, conventions, laws, institutions, etc., of the national state, which are the embodiment of the national spirit. It cannot be repeated too often that this position of Hegel's is mainly due, on the one hand, to the inspiration which he drew from the glories of Hellas, and on the other hand to the historical situation of Europe at that time. Germany was then at a crisis in her fate. Hegel proposes to save his nation from foreign invasion by the formation of a strong state, and so he holds to Absolute Ethicality in the life of fatherland and for the nation. Individualism is to him pernicious, whereas humanitarianism or cosmopolitanism is vague and utopian.

On the whole, Hegel's insistence upon the superiority of the ethical norm of the nation-state is just. For the *ethos* of the nation-state is the synthesis of all the achievements of mankind throughout all ages, so far as they have been appropriated by the nation. Compared with the spirit of the Age in the universal history whose range is world-wide, the national-spirit has the advantage of intensity and vivacity; while in comparison with the private conscience of individuals, it is universal and mediated.

The spirit of the nation, according to Hegel, has Right to a certain type of life, to an independent national culture. The forms of ritual, manners, disciplines, morals, customs, traditions, conventions, institutions, etc., as forms of the self-determination of the nation, as derived from this Right, are the content of the freedom of the nation. Individuals have no title to any peculiar mode of life ; their rights are already articulated within the content of Right. In the well-organized nation-state, Hegel urges[1] *conformity* to the national discipline, traditions, morals, customs, laws, institutions, etc., as against the dictates of private, individual conscience. Individuals can claim no more than to have the laws explicitly promulgated so that they may know what is right, and to be brought to understand the meaning of institutions, traditions, etc., so that they personally may appropriate them anew, or have them " inwardized." Private conscience can be allowed to have its own convictions only in so far as these do not oppose the existing ethicality. It is, according to Hegel ,[2] only in times when the established morality or adopted ethical principles of the actual world are so shallow, unspiritual, and shadowy as to be incapable of satisfying the better will, that philosophers like Socrates, the Stoics, etc., are forced to seek within themselves, and to determine out of their own minds, truer forms of right and good.

When the content of Ethics is conceived as conformity of the individual to the duties of the situation in which he finds himself, it is

---

1. See Phil. of Right, sect. 132.
2. See *ibid.*, sect. 138.

rectitude or integrity.[1]   But when its reflection or manifestation in the individual is ascribed to the peculiar character of the individual, it is *virtue*.   Rectitude is, Hegel tells us,[2] the universal norm of conduct in an ethical community where what man should do, what duties he must fulfil, are determined and known ; whereas virtue, in the Greek sense of *excellence,* is exceptional.   Virtue rests on the nature of particularly gifted individuals.   It belongs, therefore, to the undeveloped states of society where ethical principles and the means to their realization have not yet been universally determined.

Moreover, the private conscience of the individual *per se* is not trustworthy.   It is particular, indefinite, wayward, capricious, and, in some cases, even egoistic.   The individual is a spiritual and rational being only potentially.   His spirituality and rationality can be developed and actualized only in the realm of Ethicality, where all the accumulated achievements of mankind are available for the evoking, expanding, disintegrating, and redintegrating of his own potentiality.   Apart from the Ethical fabric, he cannot even have a conscience.   To have a Good Will, one must know what is good.   Now, his view of Goodness, no matter whether it be valid or invalid, is shaped or moulded by the cultural environment in which he finds himself, and to which he is so closely tied that he cannot get away from it.   " Except as a member of a Nation-state, the individual is not himself, has no reality and truth, and cannot live an ethical life." [3]

The attempt to annul all objective standards, and to trust to petty individualistic conviction is very dangerous.   The eighteenth-century moral theory of subjective conscience, when tried by experiment in France, resulted in the Reign of Terror ; [4] for everybody regards what is approved by his own conscience as exclusively good and right, although in point of fact, it may be decisively bad and wrong.   Indeed, no current form of morality or norm of conduct is absolutely true and final,

1.   See Phil. of Right, sect. 150.
2.   See *ibid.*
3.   Phil. of Right, sect. 258.
4.   See Hegel : Phil. of History, Bohn's ed., pp. 461 – 472.

and individuals have on this very account to do their share in promoting the ethical attainments of the nation. But to achieve progress, it is necessary to have reached it ; to destroy a law it is necessary to have fulfilled it. Mere *Aufklärung* is synonymous with *Ausklärung*. A thorough-going individualism of natural rights is untenable ; its logical outcome would be anarchism and, consequently, unconditional submission to despotism when the weariness of casuistry is felt, and the catastrophe of caprice has become manifest. Nor, on the other hand, does the Spirit of the Age in universal history furnish an efficient moral standard. It is, indeed, common to all human creatures of the time ; but for this very reason it is very attenuated. As compared with the national Spirit, it has no vital bearing on the daily life of individuals, and, therefore, can take no grasp of their minds. The reason is quite plain. The individual members of a nation have their racial characteristics and other traits, due to geographical and climatic circumstances, which are not common to them with other peoples. And as they have lived a common life with each other for hundreds or thousands of years, they inevitably form among themselves intimate relations in which aliens cannot share ; and in these relations alone do they find satisfaction and fellowship. Hence a world-wide norm of moral life could not be adequate to their moral disposition. It may not be foreign to them, but it is superficial and so cannot permeate the depths of their minds. Unity, secured by the spirit of an Age, which cannot take possession of the minds of individuals, will soon turn to indifference.[1] Furthermore, the spirit of the Age is *vague*. In order to make itself effective and accessible, it must be expressed through the " vehicle " of nations or individuals. But if any " dominant nation " or " celebrated individuals " be recognized as the representatives of the universal spirit of the Age, as Hegel suggested,[2] the spirit would be thereby particularized — i. e., nationalized or individualized, and cease to be the true spirit of the Age.

---

1. It is because of the same reason that no religion has, as yet, succeeded in becoming universal ; although attempts have been made through military expeditions, missionary enterprise and other activities.
2. See Phil. of Spirit, sections, 549, 550.

So far Hegel's insistence on the ethical norm of the nation-state is defensible. But as a reaction against eighteenth-century individualism and as a reflection of the Hellenic glories, his presentation inevitably over-emphasized the group side so as to lose the individual in the universal. The truth is that the relation between the individual and the nation group is as follows: the individual has no meaning without being a member of the nation-state; and the latter, on the other hand, has no existence apart from the individual members. In a word, the individual is caught in a dilemma or contradiction, he has to maintain the *ethos* of the nation; that is, conform to the ethical norms of the nation-state. But he must not do this slavishly. He should appropriate the norms afresh so as to make them a unity of both *pathos* and *ethos*. In other words, he must interpret the norms in his own way, and apply them in specific cases. Such a reaction to the established norms is not destructive but rather constructive or reconstructive. That is to say, in so doing the individual has contributed to the common stock, because he has furnished some new materials and new ways of looking at the problem which, when purged through mediation, stated in a general form and recognized as essential, may serve to enlarge, enrich, deepen, and improve the content of the life of the group. In this way moral progress is carried on. Nonconformity leads to Anarchism, which is, of course, blameworthy. But mere conformity, on the other hand, results in conventionalism. It prevents variety of life. In this way the process of moral evolution will become crystallized. And if any ethical norm becomes stereotyped, and meantime no breath of fresh spirit blow, its vitality will pass away, and formalism, or its alternative, disorganization, will result.

In principle Hegel is aware of this.[1] He insists vigorously upon self-consciousness as an essential factor in the development of spiritual freedom. To him, unconscious acceptance of any ethical norm, like implicit faith in any religious creed, is nothing but spiritual slavery. And in one passage in the Philosophy of Right he expressly says that

1. See Phil. of Right, sections 12 and 142 and Phil. of Spirit sect. 552.

the ethical has to attain to its knowledge, volition and actualization through the self-consciousness and activity of the individual.[1] But presently elsewhere in the same work he says, " The individual is related to the universal (the nation-state) as something accidental: whether the individual exists or not is indifferent to the objective Ethicality which alone is abiding.[2] This sounds precisely like Platonic or Mediæval Realism. And in his recommendation of "rectitude" as the universal norm of conduct in an ethical community, and in his disparagement of virtue as the norm of undeveloped state of society, he cannot but evoke those criticisms which accused him of burking the individual, of taking the existing reality as final, of worshipping a brutal Actualism, etc. The present state of society cannot be said to be completely developed. Even if we do not think that this is an Age of decadence, it is surely not the Golden Age. So long as development goes on, philosophers of Socrates' type and virtue (in the sense of *excellence*) are always needed. Mere conformity, as Hegel's " rectitude " implies, would make the process stagnant. The formulated norms are, after all, the average requirements of average men for the time being. They have only temporary validity. And if the process is to be completed at all, it can be done only by the virtuous reformers rather than by the mere law-abiding good citizens. Indeed, virtue may have the permanent characteristic of imperfection; to feel that you have done well implies that you have not done wholly well. But " rectitude " in the sense of conformity may be fulfilled without any real virtue at all. Hegel's statement contradicts the principles which he otherwise presupposes. This unguarded self-contradiction can be excused only by the historical situation of that time.

However, that is not all. The domination of Hegel's mind then by the idea of the salvation of Germany from foreign invasion through the formation of a united strong nation-state, and his impatience over the vague ideals of Romanticist humanitarianism or cosmopolitanism, and

1. See sect. 142.
2. See sect. 145.

over the shallow and pretentious emotionalism of the "demagogic folk," have led him to emphasize the nation-state to such an extent as to make it in some ways individualistic, antagonistic, and imperious to its fellow-nations, and isolated from the evolutionary process of universal history. The position of the nation in universal history, just like that of the individual in the nation-state, is subject to a dilemma or contradiction. It has right to an unimpeded development and free expression along certain characteristic lines; for only in this way can it be really productive and contributory to the common stock of human civilization. A stereotyped uniformity means a dead level. But, after all, the outlook and capacity of national culture are limited; any national culture forms only a particular step or stage in the movement of the "liberation" of Spiritual Substance. Thus a nation can occupy one grade and accomplish only one task in the whole liberating process. Accordingly the achievements produced by national characteristics must be subjected to a mediation with other nations, and also to the judgment of the whole dialectic process of universal history. In other words, the national spirit must keep in contact in terms of give-and-take with the current spiritual movements among all nations and ages in the universal history, and not live secluded from them. Otherwise the national culture will be left stationary, if not turned backward.

In principle Hegel is no particularist; he makes no objection to such considerations, nor is he ignorant of them. This is plainly seen in the sections 548, 549, 552 of the Philosophy of Spirit. But in the Philosophy of Right[1] he says, "The spirit of a nation, the *Athene*, is the divine that knows and wills itself." "The state is the actuality of the Ethical-Idea, is the march of God on earth." "The State in and for itself is the Ethical Totality, the actualization of freedom which is the Absolute end of Reason." And in his early System of Ethicality[2] he lays it down that the national unity is the supreme appearance of the Eternal and

1. Sections 257, 258.
2. See Wallace: Hegel's Phil. of Mind, p. 153.

Absolute; even though the divine may expand the limited national spirit till it becomes a Spirit of universal history. Again in another place[1] he also regards the State as a single individual exclusive of other like individuals. All these expressions sound like watchwords of orthodox Nationalism. And even when he is insisting upon universal history as the paramount step towards the 'liberation' of Spirit, he still says,[2] "The self-consciousness of a particular nation is a vehicle for the contemporary development of the collective Spirit in its actual existence; it is the objective actuality in which that spirit for the time being invests its will. Against this Absolute will the other particular national spirits have no rights; that nation dominates the world." If we take such statements in their isolation, the universalism which he posited in the last part of the Division on Objective Spirit and elaborated in his Philosophy of History would seem merely a nationalism universalized.[3] In more concrete terms, it would spell the imposition of one particular national culture upon others, or the conquest of all other cultures by one nation; but not a mediation of all cultures. Hence the recent ascription of the doctrine of *Kultur* directly to Hegel is not altogether without justification.

In a section[4] of the Philosophy of Right he says, " In dealing with the Idea of the State, we must not have before our eyes a particular state, or a particular institution; we must rather study the Idea." Very well. This is just what we should expect of him and also expresses exactly the attitude we ought to take in any study. But in point of fact, it is impracticable. In humanistic studies especially, no individual can entirely transcend the interests of the particular group to which he belongs and with which he is so closely related that anything which affects its destiny reacts inevitably upon him. Fichte started as a cosmopolitan; but after the battle of Jena in 1806 he became the most

1. Phil. of Spirit, sect. 545.
2. *Ibid.*, sect. 550. See before, pp. 70, 71.
3. Cf. before pp. 21, 22.
4. Sect. 258.

vigorous of Nationalists.[1] Hegel, who also was born and brought up in Swabia, may be more shrewd than his compatriot, but, when involved in the same environment and confronted by the same situation, he loses something of his 'hard-headedness.' Inevitably he was affected by contemporary events. It was impossible for him to follow inflexibly the principle which he laid down before himself. This is the chief influence which clouded the rationality of his philosophy and made him untrue to himself.

1. Cf. Adamanson, Fichte.

CHAPTER VIII

METAPHYSICAL BACKGROUND AND SOME APPLICATIONS IN HEGEL'S ETHICS

As has been mentioned in the first chapter of the present work, Hegel in his Treatise on Natural Right emphatically insisted that no science can be treated independently of Metaphysics. This principle he faithfully followed throughout his philosophical life. From the foregoing pages it is plain that he made frequent use of his metaphysical principles as the background of his ethical position. To the present writer's mind, Hegel is perfectly right. As has been said in the foregoing chapters, especially in the directly preceding one, the Ethical life can be achieved only through the medium of the objective, the natural and social world. It is, so to speak, the formation of a new reality in Nature. But such formation is in fact nothing but the fulfilment and completion of the promise and implication of Nature and the actualization of the potentialities of Man, or the realization of the essential nature of mankind. Such fulfilment and completion, actualization or realization are initiated, nay, motived, by the world of Aspiration or the realm of Absolute Spirit, and carried out by human thoughts and activities or Man's interpretation of ultimate Reality and intelligent conduct in socialized living, and accomplished through a constructive mediation of human Spirit with the realm of Nature on the one hand, and with the realm of Aspiration on the other, so as to bring all the three realms, the natural, social and aspirational, wherein Man lives, into intelligible and harmonious relationship, and thereby help to effect the perfection of the Universe as a Whole.

From this standpoint, it is self-evident, that an Ethical theory must have a metaphysical background if it is to be adequate at all. The reason is quite plain. To achieve an ethical life, the first preliminary requisite is to have a sound view of life, to take an appropriate

107

attitude towards it, and choose the right way to accomplish the same. When this first requisite is wanting, all efforts which are made to attain the pre-conceived ideal simply result in a collapse. But here arise at once the questions: What is the sound view of life? What is the proper attitude towards it? What ·is the right way to accomplish the same? Why should one view of life rather than another be adopted? Why should this rather than another attitude towards it be taken? Why should this way rather than another be chosen? Such questions can be answered only in terms of the true nature of Man, the constitution of the Universe as a Whole, the place of Man therein, and the vocation of man and the possibility of his achieving it. In other words, a valid Ethical ideal must find justification and explanation in a metaphysical system. The classical expression of this may be found in Geulincx. [1] His aphorism reads: "Know yourself, know from what you are, your true relation to the world, and hence, your destiny in the world." [2]

Moreover, the universe is a system of reason and law; voluntarism finds no room for manifestation there. The natural world is plastic, but not chaotic or formless. It is susceptible of spiritual ideals, but only in accordance with its nature and potentiality. In other words, it can be transformed, but only in a definite manner, not at random. The ethical subject may claim that its purposes, intentions and higher aims be realized in the world. But the world sets up a counter-claim that its order be understood and respected. So a true view of ethical life and a sane attitude towards it and the right way to accomplish it can be attained only through a complete mediation with the universe. Or, what amounts to the same thing, since ethical life is to be achieved in the universe and in connection with all the

---

1. The value of his philosophy as a whole does not concern us here. Plato and Aristotle may be said to have held the same position, whereas the Stoic and Epicurean Ethics are distinctly based on their metaphysical doctrines. But it is, so far as I know, Geulincx who first plainly stated this. Subsequently Spinoza, Hegel and T. H. Green are the most prominent exponents of this view.
2. See K. Fischer: History of Mod. Phil., Vol. I, Bk. III, Ch. 3.

various moments or factors thereof, an adequate ethical theory must needs take a full account of, and pay due respect to, the constitution of the Universe as a whole *and* the characteristics of, and the relations between, the various moments or factors of it. It is silly to dream of something which, in the nature of the case, cannot possibly be realized in the world; and thus to fall into despair, or to be forced to content oneself with the self-deceptive satisfaction of taking copper for gold, as in the naïve optimism or pseudo-idealism of the Romanticists. On the other hand, it is equally silly to lament the imperfections in the world and thus forfeit the possibility of completing it and the opportunity of living a virtuous life therein, as in the self-negating pessimism of some Determinists. All these mischiefs are, to the writer's judgment, simply due to a lack or mistake of metaphysical basis in the formation of ethical theory.

Metaphysics does not of itself prescribe any ethical theory, but it exercises enormous influence in the formation and selection of one. In the first place, it furnishes a number of principles of which Ethics must needs make use in the formation of its theory. But these principles are so fundamental and complicated that Ethics cannot develop them by its own capacity. Secondly, a comprehension of the constitution of the Universe as a whole and an insight into the nature of ultimate Reality may suggest the possibility of some novel ethical order and arouse aspiration to a higher spirituality. In this way some newer view of life is shaped; a truer attitude towards it is gradually evolved, and the right way towards it is indicated. And thirdly, an ethical theory which finds justification in metaphysical truth, may be thereby corroborated and made more powerful and enduring. On the other hand, what is found inconsistent with it will thereby be invalidated and lose its hold on men. For what is in knowledge found contradictory to the nature of ultimate Reality will no longer take hold of human mind in conduct.

The influence Metaphysics exercises in the formation and selection of ethical theories is, at first, not easy to apprehend. For one's conception and interpretation of, and insight into, the nature of ultimate Reality, as a rule, comes to mould one's view of, and attitude towards, life and one's way to accomplish it only by implication. It is only when we encounter some difficulty regarding the soundness, sanity and validity of such a view, such an attitude and such a method that an explicit appeal and reference to Metaphysics for explanation and endorsement becomes urgent.

However, that Metaphysics exercises such influence is sure, though not apparent on the surface. The reason is not at all strange. Human Experience is an organic whole. A man cannot split himself into several parts, and so make one part of himself inconsistent with and contradictory to the other. Volition is motivated by feeling and guided by intelligence. The Kantian dualism between knowledge and action, between the " Pure Reason " and " Practical Reason " is an unfortunate misconception. Kant maintains this position simply because he does not go through the whole course of the intellectual dialectic process; so that his first two Critiques have little bearing upon one another. In other philosophical systems it may be observed that an Idealist ethics is likely to seek its ideal in the complete realization of the true nature of Man; and hence in the perfection of the Whole, of which the ethical subject or moral agent forms a moment, and wherein he has significance exactly in proportion to his merit and contribution. A Realist ethics may find congenial expression in hedonism or utilitarianism, which, to the Oriental mind, is no ethics at all. And a Pragmatist ethics, if any be possible, is destined to result in casuistry and moral corruption — not to say bankruptcy — if its logical implications are fully carried out. This shows clearly that *Lebensanschauung* can never be free from the influence of *Weltanschauung*.

Among contemporary writers, Dr. G. E. Moore is the most convinced anti-metaphysical Ethicist. [1] But, to my judgement, this is simply due to his misunderstanding of the nature of Goodness. To him, the predicate " good," which, he maintains, is the unique notion peculiar to Ethics, is indefinable. It cannot be referred to another category, nor be analysed into elements. It is a simple notion just as yellow or blue

---

1. See his Principia Ethica; esp. Chap. IV.

is a simple notion. [1] Everybody can see it or experience it in case it is present. Hence Ethics can be separated from other departments of study. But this is not at all true. For what is " good " to a Hedonist may not be so to a Rigorist. " Good " to a Mussulman may not be so to a Christian. " Good " to a cultivated German may not be so to a *Kriegsschieber*. And the barbarian, who has no view of life, or one which is entirely different from that of the civilized peoples, cannot possibly see a highly spiritual " good " when this is suggested to him, although he may learn to see yellow and blue easily. Dr. Moore admits that Metaphysics may serve an ethical purpose, in suggesting things which would not otherwise have occurred to us, but which, when they are suggested, we see to be good. [2] But here one truth which is latent but paramountly important, has escaped Dr. Moore's notice. That is, we see certain things, suggested to us, to be good, simply because we find them fitted to our scale of valuation. But this scale always involves, implicitly or explicitly, a *Lebensanschauung* and, in turn, a *Weltanschauung*, however inchoate, vague and inconsistent these may be. In other words, Metaphysics, through its influence over our view of life, not only serves to suggest moral ideals, but also serves to determine them. Dr. Moore's own conception of " good " as reported here, and his discussion of utilitarianism in his small volume entitled " Ethics," themselves, perhaps contrary to Dr. Moore's intention, are the best evidence that one's ethical position is inevitably moulded by one's metaphysical standpoint. Dr. Moore further maintains that, as a source of suggestions, Fiction can serve Ethics more effectively than Metaphysics. [3] But, to my mind, a metaphysical truth may lead to a real view of life and an earnest attitude towards it, whereas Fiction as Fiction cannot produce such an effect.

It is true that, as the Empiricist ethicist says, we cannot wait until Metaphysics has given a final verdict upon the riddle of the Universe before a study of Ethics is undertaken. And in sympathy with this, we

1. See Principia Ethica, Chap. I.
2. See *Ibid.*, p. 121.
3. See *Ibid.*

may add that in the history of human life the practical as a rule confronts us before the theoretical. But as soon as Man has leisure to reflect, [1] the theoretical immediately exerts a powerful influence upon him. And even in dealing with practical problems of moral life, there is always *something* which plays a rôle similar to that of Metaphysics, so far as it serves to give justification for the preservation of certain moral values, and offers some hint as to the possibility of completion in a larger and more ideal order. In primitive societies, mythology, immemorial legend, uncriticized beliefs, etc., did this work, however lacking in real basis they may have been. [2] But, on the other hand, we must admit that any form of good conduct and any truly valuable element of moral life detected and enunciated by intuition and immediate sense of feeling may help to discover and build up metaphysical truth, although here the final determining function is still with Metaphysics. So the question ultimately comes to be one of comparative importance in the process of mutual modification. Taken together, they may contribute to one another. The new truth found in one is naturally destined to effect an augmentation and re-organization of the other. The question of historical priority depends upon our point of view, and is barren, because, unimportant.

However, some Empiricist ethicists hold that, as modern Anthropology shows, all the values or "goods" with which Ethics is concerned, are developed in the historico-social life of men and disclosed to our knowledge by empirical methods of "trial and error," observation and experiment, or the casual success of a happy stroke, but are not derived or deduced from any metaphysical theorizing. Such a position is perhaps simply a case of the "question-begging" fallacy. In the first place it forgets the fact that such a development of moral values in history has been made possible by the implicit orientation of an

---

1. See Aristotle : Metaphysics, Bk. 1.
2. It should be understood, however, that mythology, legend, etc., are able to perform this function only on account of the state of knowledge possessed by primitive peoples. As soon as they are seen to be what they are, they lose their influence at once.

unconsciously presupposed end.   In other words, there subsists in the mind of man a general and, perhaps, vague idea (*Vorstellung*) that the Universe as a whole, or human life in particular, is to be converted into a rational and harmonious whole, or at least destined to become so. This presupposed end serves as the determining standard by which we can detect and select values which would have otherwise been missed or wrongly rejected.   Such a presupposed end has been the final aim of Metaphysics.   It is oftentimes forgotten and is brought to explicit consciousness with difficulty simply because it is so fundamental and obvious that it is silently taken for granted.   Or, look at the matter from the other side, we take it for granted without taking the trouble to reflect upon it, or assume it as a matter of course without being always aware of it.   Secondly, the doctrine in question also overlooks the fact that even empirical " trial and error," observation and analysis, etc., would be impossible without the presupposition that human life and the Universe in general are orderly, rational and intelligible, and also the presupposition that there exists a self which is identical, consistent, intelligent, and has organizing power.   And these presuppositions are just those difficult problems which can be illuminated only by metaphysical discussion.

The Empiricist ethicists still may urge that Ethics may assume the ultimate principles of Metaphysics without defining, investigating, criticizing and validating them ; and may accept the existing moral order, and confine itself to the observation and analysis of the facts of moral life without attempting to explain why there should be such a moral order in the world.   This will do, I admit, as a temporary measure, especially when the thinking world is tired of metaphysical speculation, and has arrived at a state of despair ; and when at the same time, the problems of daily life also press hard for solution.   But as soon as the practical problems are disposed of, and the thinking intelligence is refreshed a little, the striving after theoretical satisfaction will assert itself immediately — not only because human beings are curious, but because our practical ethical creed must have a theoretical foundation.   Otherwise when antagonists propound antithetic ethical theories and press for acceptation of them, when the Sceptic raises questions as to the possibility of an ethical life and the study of Ethics as a science, or when the Nihilist wants to know the basis and necessity of the existence of an ethical order in general, we shall find ourselves helpless. 'And when such a controversy arises, a dogmatic solution is unavailing, while an agnostic silence is suicidal. In other words, a resort to Metaphysics for explanation and support will be found necessary. The ethical teaching of Confucius is thoroughly practical, but his pupils, grandson and other disciples had to develop it into a theoretical architectonic. Similarly the Christian fathers and the mediæval Schoolmen and the Brahminists have formulated, on the Gospels of their prophets, magnificent metaphysical systems. In modern times, the moral difficulties which impelled Spinoza to a speculative inquiry, as he tells us in his Treatise on the Improvement of Understanding, furnish us with a good example of the proof of our contention.

The foregoing pages of the present chapter have been devoted to the discussion of the legitimacy, nay, the necessity of a metaphysical background for the orientation and explanation of Ethical life in general. Now we may come to consider the correctness or incorrectness of Hegel's application of it to Ethics. The specific principles which Hegel made use of frequently in his ethical writings are: (1) the unity of the real and the rational, or of the ideal and the actual; (2) the unity of the inward and the outward, or of the subjective and the objective ; and (3) the universality of " Dialectic " in the finite world. The meaning of the first has been expounded in Chapter VI, and there the genesis of this position in Hegel's Ethics, and also the metaphysical ground, have been traced out and the difficulties explained, objections answered and short-comings pointed out. The second has been discussed, so far as is necessary for our purpose, in the middle part of Chapter VI, and again, at length, in the first part of the preceding one. The third has been slightly touched upon in the last part of Chapter VI but a closer examination, as has been mentioned there, will be undertaken here. Generally all the applications Hegel made are defensible. But in regard to the " Dialectic," there are points upon which he should have been more discriminating and iudicious. That is, sufficient allowance must be made for the differences between the nature and modes of " Dialectic " in Metaphysics and Dialectic in the Ethical life.

Metaphysics has for its object the universe as a Whole. It deals, therefore, with the infinite as well as with the finite ; and anything finite is treated by it as being part of the process of Dialectic. Accordingly, the terms which carry on the dialectic process there are utterly heterogeneous in character. To take the final stage, which is the most adequate of all, of the Dialectic as an example for discussion, the triad in that case consists of : (1) the Subjective Notion, or the rational aspect of Reality, as the Thesis ; (2) Object, or the real aspect of Reality, i. e., Nature in the ordinary sense of the term, as the antithesis ; (3) the Absolute Idea, or the unity of Notion and Objectivity, or of the real and the rational, as the Synthesis. It is obvious that the first two terms of the triad here are diametrically antithetic to each other. It is true that the Object has in itself something of the ideal nature of the subjective Notion ; that is to say, Nature is the reflex, the outward manifestation of Intelligence, and in virtue of this characteristic, it is intelligible. But after all, Nature is, even at its best, Intelligence petrified ; it is the intelligible bound in the sensible. It never gets beyond the stage of glimpse and fragment — indications and implications of Intelligence. Nay, it is a rough and fragile receptacle, which, on account of its inefficiency to manifest the ideal principle, has led Hegel to decry it as impotent. Accordingly, the " Dialectic " movement between these terms must be particularly slow, awkward and incomplete.

Ethics, on the other hand, deals with the moral life only, that is, a comparatively small, but preponderantly spiritual portion of the whole process of the universe. In this portion, or moment rather, the principle of Dialectic may hold good just as it does in the whole process, since there certainly exist life, movement and something which comes or is carried into effect.[1] The Dialectic here, however, is through and through internal and spiritual. It may be viewed as threefold. The main Dialectic takes place between the institutional and elementary aspect of life, where Abstract Right and Law determine our acts and

---

1. See Hegel's Encycl., sect. 81.

transactions, as the thesis ; and the reflective and self-conscious aspect of life, where individual conscience serves as the criterion of conduct, as the antithesis. These resolve themselves into the unity of them both, i. e., in Ethicality, which is both institutional and self-conscious, as the Synthesis. These main terms here, however, all have their Sub-dialectic. For instance, under Ethicality, there is the sub-dialectic of Family as the Thesis, Civic Society as the antithesis, and State as the Synthesis. And the terms of the Sub-dialectic, again, have their Under-subdialectic. For instance, under State, Dialectic is at work between Internal Polity or Constitutional Law as the Thesis, External Polity or International Law as the Antithesis, and Universal History or the Rational Continuous Development of Universal Spirit as the Synthesis. Now, the most important thing to notice here is that, in these Dialectics, the terms carrying on the process are more or less homogeneous in character; for they are all modes of spiritual life. Laws and institutions, because they are imperative and impersonal, may be *prima facie* looked on as a foreign authority, imposed upon us from without, and set over against us. But as a matter of fact, they are essentially the expressions of ourselves, are the embodiment of our Spirit. So the degree of congruity or likeness of these terms is much higher than that of the terms of Metaphysical Dialectic. These terms may mediate with one another more easily, intelligently, smoothly and profoundly than the terms of the Metaphysical Dialectic, which can mediate only slowly and with difficulty, and in the end attain a success which is only partial.

Hegel did not insist upon this difference ; we may even say, he was not aware of it. A careful insistence upon such clear distinctions, which Hegel should have made, is not merely a matter of theoretical accuracy. It has practical significance as well. For an indefinite analogy, such as Hegel employed, may occasion grave misunderstanding. In particular, it may arouse the suspicion that the laws and institutions of the group life are just as external to us as nature is ; and that the mediation between the individual conscience on the one hand and the laws and institutions on the other, is just as difficult and incomplete as that between man and nature or between " notion " and "objectivity." And the mediations or dialectic movements between family and civic society, and between one nation and other nations, may also be suspected of presenting the same phenomenon, although in point of fact they are closely connected and internally related. Such a misunderstanding gives rise to some degree of irrelevant and unnecessary antagonism between the parties concerned in the ethical Dialectic.

Another difference between the Dialectic in Metaphysics and the Dialectic in Ethics, which Hegel should have made, is that which Senator Benedetto Croce has rightly pointed out in his "What is Living and What is Dead of the Philosophy of Hegel";[1] I mean the difference between the Dialectic of the synthesis of opposite abstractions of Reality and the Dialectic of the connection or relation of distinct degrees or modes of life. For instance, Being and Not-Being or Essence and Appearance, are opposite abstractions, whereas Right and Morality, Family and Society, etc., are distinct degrees or modes of life. In the Dialectic of the synthesis of opposite abstractions, e. g., Being and Not-Being, Essence and Appearance are, when taken out of relation to Becoming or Actuality, not concrete concepts. They never exist as Being and Not-Being, or Essence and Appearance, distinct from one another. Being without Not-Being, Essence without Appearance, and *vice versa*, are opposite falsities. Their truth is their synthesis Becoming, or Actuality.

On the other hand, in the Dialectic of the connection or relation of distinct degrees or modes of life, Right and Morality, Family and Society, Internal Constitution and International Polity, etc., are concrete concepts. They are the concept of Spirit considered in its various distinct determinations, not in its abstractions. Right and Morality without Ethicality, Society without Family on the one hand, and without State on the other, Nation apart from Nation Group and Universal History, are false conceptions, but not falsities which are annulled in a higher category. In other words, Right, Morality, Family, Society, etc., can exist distinctly although not separately from their equal and more adequate modes of life. They are not indifferent nor opposite to each other, but stand in a relation of higher and lower

1. For this point I am greatly indebted to Senator Croce.

degree. These degrees or modes must be unified in their distinction. For they all are expressions of Objective Spirit. And this Spirit in its self-distinction will maintain its unity, but will not be cut into pieces. However, in this interweaving, the transition from the lower degree to the higher, or from one to another, does not in any case arise, either from the bosom of the lower or from any one itself. For there is no self-contradiction in these degrees. Right does not contradict itself as Right, Family does not contradict itself as Family, etc. So the transition does not arise from any contradiction, but from the eternal nature of Spirit itself, which wants to differentiate itself by a movement internal to itself.

Hegel should have made it clear that the Dialectic in Ethics is of a different kind from that in Metaphysics. The failure to make such difference plain may entail various misunderstandings. In the first place, it may be imagined that when Ethicality, for example, is reached, Right and Morality should disappear. But, as a matter of fact, these are essential moments in the Ethical life, and the Spirit must continue to live in and through all degrees and modes, the lower as well as the higher. Secondly it may be conceived that in the organization of National State, Family and Society are lost, or condemned to annihilation. But in fact, they are preserved as dependent, while suppressed as independent. And in actual life, nobody can say that when a State-organization is inaugurated, we can be satisfied to live without Family and Civic relations. Thirdly, it may be supposed that between Internal Constitution and International Polity there is just such an antithesis and contest as there is between Being and Not-Being, etc., which are incompatible and must resolve themselves in a third term. But, in reality, Internal Constitution and International Polity are closely related and both must mediate with one another and so conduce equally to the continuous development of Universal Spirit.

It seems exceedingly strange that so thorough and systematic a thinker as Hegel can, in some respects, be so incautious as to conceive the connection of degrees to be of the same kind as the synthesis of opposite abstractions. But in point of fact, "it was," as Senator Croce says, [1] "almost inevitable that this should be so, owing to the peculiar psychological condition in which the discoverer of a new aspect of the real finds himself (in this case, the synthesis of opposites). He is so tyrannized over by his own discovery, so inebriated with the new wine of that truth, as to see it everywhere before him, and to be led to conceive everything according to the new formula. . . . To discern the differences between the two theories was reserved for a later historical period, when the new wine was matured and settled."

In connection with the application of the doctrine of Dialectic, another difficulty has arisen in Hegel's ethical writings. The Dialectic requires a triad or triplicity of thesis, antithesis and synthesis; otherwise the principle has no application. But there are cases where the triplicity is lacking or is not clearly present, and yet our philosopher is fond of applying his doctrine universally. Consequently, in such cases, he is forced to create a triad. But this is artificial, and caused him much trouble. In the "Phenomenology of Spirit" there are apparently six degrees or steps of Consciousness, Self-consciousness, Reason, Spirit, Religion and Absolute Knowledge at hand. This does not fit the Dialectic. But Hegel divided them into two classes marked respectively with one or two letters. It might have been hoped that hereby two triads could be formed out of the six terms. However Hegel found Reason constituting at once the last step C. of the first class and the commencing step (AA) of the second class. So following the triad A. B. C., a quadruple (AA) (BB) (CC) (DD) was formed. K. Fischer tried to relieve the difficulty by treating A. B. (DD) as the main triad, with C. (AA) (BB) (CC) as the sub-triad, which forms a prelude to Absolute Knowledge and at the same time presents a process of dialectic. [2] But we cannot be assured that this is Hegel's scheme. In the "Philosophy of Spirit," Spirit is divided into (1) Subjective, (2) Objective, (3) Absolute. But as a matter of

1. *Op. cit.*, pp. 95, 96.
2. See *op. cit.*, pp. 306, 307.

fact, the division can be only a relative one. The modes of Spirit are not so clear-cut and logically distinct. Hence it is very difficult, or rather impossible, to draw a hard and fast line between them. For example, the development of free mind and will which according to Hegel's scheme belongs to Subjective Spirit, has much to do with, and so reaches out into, the realm of Objective Spirit; [1] whereas the Objective Spirit, when it culminates in Universal Spirit, has surreptitiously entered the realm of Absolute Spirit. And the Absolute Spirit, on the other hand, can be attained only through the Subjective and Objective. In other words, these steps or modes can only be viewed as implications, not as elements of a classification. And it is also worth noticing here that in the " Phenomenology of Spirit," " Spirit," which in the " Philosophy of Spirit " lies within the realm of Objective Spirit," is put on the same level with Religion and Absolute Knowledge, i. e., elevated into the realm of Absolute Spirit; while the Æsthetic Spirit is totally absent. Again, in the "Philosophy of History" the method of triplicity is found incapable of handling the material. A quadruplicity of Oriental world, Greek world, Roman world, and Germanic world comes upon the stage; and here our philosopher had to give up his triplicity.

1. See before, p. 95.

CHAPTER IX

SOME SPECIFIC PROBLEMS IN HEGEL'S ETHICAL TEACHING

The last three chapters have been devoted to a critical appreciation of the general characteristics and guiding principles of Hegel's Ethics. Now we turn to specific points of his teaching. Since Professor Reyburn's work has been so thorough and admirable in this respect, I think it would be superfluous to repeat what he has done. Accordingly I shall take up here only those problems which I find still in need of discussion. Such a critique as I propose to offer here cannot avoid fragmentariness, and the selection of the points to be discussed cannot be more than a matter of preference. But, as the situation stands, I found it impossible to do otherwise.

Hegel's treatment of Property as the first primary and necessary step of the self-realization of Will may be regarded as giving a sound basis to the existence of property, whereby it has not only utility but moral value as well. So long as human nature stands, and man first realizes himself in the appropriation of natural things, Property is and will remain an essential institution. Communism, which seeks to abolish it, is occupied with the solution of the economical problem only; the ethical issue in it has not yet attracted its attention. Again the appropriation of this rather than that natural thing already implies a view of life; if Communism is to be anything more than a materialistic dead level, it must find some means of replacing this function of property before it is ready to abolish it. However, the writer is not to be understood as unsympathetic to the Socialist complaint of injustice in the distribution of wealth; what he insists upon is that a man is more than a mere consumer of material goods; he has some higher aim. The problem of distribution therefore cannot be solved separately, but must be attacked in connection with the other basic problems of life.

121

Hegel's insistence on subjective self-consciousness as a necessary stage, but not more than a stage, in the whole development of freedom, is very important. Certainly mere observance of conventional morality means spiritual slavery, while mere Conscience or Good Will is liable to introduce anarchism, if not subjected to the mediation of Ethicality.

It is a curious thing that Hegel's Ethics in regard to the Family is in one sense over-romantic despite the fact that Hegelianism has been charged with over-intellectualism. The validity of his view of the family as a unity of feeling, in contrast to the State which is a unity of Law and self-conscious intelligence, is very questionable. To the writer's judgement, the feeling of Love in a well-founded family, just as in a well-established State, has been corroborated by intelligent insight. That is to say, the family régime has, *after reflection*, been recognized as the proper way of living a rational life. In this sense, the feeling is no longer mere feeling, but is transformed into intelligence or intellectual love.

To Hegel the realm of family comprises two generations only, that is, the married couple with their children. This circle is independent of the parents of the married couple, i. e., it constitutes a new family without the parents as component factors. The reason he virtually gave for this is, that the real substance of the family is ethical Love, instead of consanguinity. Now, the feeling of love, Hegel thinks, cannot permeate through an extensive stock. In an extended range of generations, if the feeling of love is not lacking, it is certainly attenuated. In such a case, Hegel urges, if a unity is insisted upon, it can comprehend only things which are external and independent of feeling — the essence of family life.

To the writer's mind, this is not wholly true. The circle of the family may be extended as far as the posterity of a common *living* head, male or female, goes. That means a union of three to five generations, varying directly with the age of the head and the quickness of reproduction. Under such a head a spiritual unity is secured very naturally because the kinship or likeness of the members has been brought to vivid consciousness by the presence of this living head. Unlike the wider clan of remote consanguinity, such a spiritual union of three to five generations under one living head, is not too big for the feeling of love to permeate. The feeling in a wide circle may, indeed, be attenuated, but if we trust to feeling exclusively, even married life would be impossible; for feeling always contains an accidental element, and is liable to fluctuation. So the truth is rather that the natural feeling has been mediated through other considerations of experience.

And even if the feeling of love be granted as the essence of family, as Hegel urges, there is no reason why this feeling should not be expanded beyond the narrow circle of the young couple. As support to this position, Hegel even goes so far as to allege that children as a rule love their parents less than parents their children; and that the children leave their parents in a sense behind them. But, in the writer's experience, this is not true. It may be true in the Occidental world where the Greek view that " the old shall be honoured or respected only when age is adorned with mature counsels and valuable wisdom," [1] still exercises enormous influence. But in the Orient, the attitude of children towards their parents is dominated by a sense of piety and gratitude; the idea of " efficiency " is not taken into account. Not that they think of their parents as ideal and so are inspired by and devoted to them; but they hold they are always indebted to them, and so must, in return, be pious and grateful, and render filial service and honour to them. They do this not as a matter of convention but out of their heart. They really feel uneasy and even heartbroken, if they in any wise fail here. Therefore, the idea of " efficiency " is no standard to determine respect and honour in this region of human relations.

From this standpoint, Hegel again falls into an over-intellectualism or rather a mood of vulgar calculation, which is characteristic of *Bourgeois* Society. His discussion shows a lack of affection and sentiment between the aged parents and the grown-up children. Admitting that the married young couple must love each other to the maximum, how could the common living ancestor afford to lose the joy

---

1. G. S. Brett, The Government of Man, p. 65.

of association with his posterity ! How could he stand the sadness of witnessing the splitting up of his ' personality ' by the dissolution of the family! When a man has had the good fortune to unite a goodly number of excellent descendants, the house is sure to be full of an atmosphere of kindness, tenderness, joy, love and affection; and all these feelings will be cordial, sincere, and frank, instead of being sophisticated, and 'institutional.' Such an extensive family is so graceful and admirable that a man who aspires to happiness cannot regard his good fortune as complete without such a family. Hegel's emphasis on the intensive love of the young couple, at the expense of a larger spiritual union, is due to a confluence of Romanticism and Hellenism. The former induces him to insist on an intensive love between the married couple, while the latter makes him allow vulgar calculation as between parents and their children. Had these two influences been mediated, intelligent insight would have penetrated into the circle of the couple, and the feeling of love would have expanded; Hegel might then have reached " absolute " truth.

Passing from the general features of the family to its first specific phase of marriage, Hegel seems to recognize the fact that feeling is not the sole basis of family life. So his discussion of marriage is much better than his discussion of the family in general. As has been pointed out in our fifth chapter, he regards marriage as legal-ethical love, that is, feeling mediated through intelligence. Such a view of marriage is very creditable. The union, a spiritual union of husband and wife, is certainly motivated by the feeling of love, and effected by the action of will. But it is through ethico-legal expressions alone that the ethical purpose of wedlock is made clear and tempered into permanency.

Hegel is also praiseworthy in showing that marriage is neither a mere sexual relation, nor a civil contract. While the feeling of love is unstable and liable to fluctuation, the natural impulse of sexual relation is still more accidental. It perishes as soon as it is satisfied. How could a permanent ethical relation be based upon such a momentary animal passion ! Civil contract, on the other hand, is a bargain entered upon by competent persons for mutual advantage. It is not so essential to them as marriage is. In contract, the parties are in spirit external to each other. They take a *casual* attitude towards the compact, which compact, therefore, can be abandoned at will. Marriage, on the contrary, is the universal will; it springs from the ideal nature of man. Such ideal nature is the universal heritage into which men are born. So it is essential *par excellence* to human life. Even when the sexual passion and the purpose of mutual advantage can be satisfied otherwise, there is still need of wedlock.

However, in some quarters of the world to-day marriage has been ' commercialized ' to some extent, that is to say, invaded by an element of contract. I do not mean that there are, in connection with marriage, some regulations concerning external facts such as dowry, means of support, etc.; but that there is a sceptical and antagonistic attitude of reserve in the inner feeling of the parties towards each other. To enter the marriage-relation in this spirit is to lose the original meaning of marriage; the element of mutual externality has slipped in. Such an implicit tragedy is altogether due to a misunderstanding of the purpose of marriage.

As to the family means or property Hegel maintains that it is essentially connected with the individual's marriage and less intimately with his original stock or house. This is (1) theoretically based upon his view that the principle of the family is ethical Love, a love in turn, pre-eminently illustrated in the intensive affection of the youthful couple. Secondly, in addition to this he alleges, from casual observation, that (2) a married couple with their children form a nucleus of their own in contrast to a more extensive house. Hence the conclusion that marriage should set up a new family which has its independent footing as against the stem or house from which it has proceeded; or that the individual's financial status must be more vitally connected with marriage than with the wider family union. [1]

The fallacy of such reasoning is obvious. It is fallacious because its premises are invalid. The invalidity of the theoretical premise has

---

1. See Philosophy of Right, sect. 172.

been pointed out in the present chapter, whereas the invalidity of the supposed factual premise may be found in its capricious individualism. The natural instinct of self-seeking must be first mitigated and transformed to higher aims through the discipline of the wider family, and then through social organization and other wider systems ; it must at any rate not be encouraged.

We may say positively that the family fortune, like the family, should not be divided till the death of the family head. The maintenance of a larger spiritual union has justification not only in the greatness of the house and the integrity of the ' personality ' of the head, but also in the fact that every member of the union gains in significance when he goes beyond the family circle and makes contact with the larger world. Furthermore, it also furnishes protection and assistance to the less talented members of the same stock, and thus makes the house as a whole more flourishing. The common objection to this is that the married couple, having reached maturity, have to assert their will, realize their individuality ; whereas under the common reign of a big house, the individuals may lose themselves. But such objection is not *prima facie* tenable. As a matter of fact, the individuals may realize themselves by rendering valuable service to promote the standing and the common good of the family, and to bestow assistance upon its members ; just as the citizen may realize himself, and build up his personality, by performing valuable duties for the good of the nation and by serving his fellowmen; but not by founding a new world apart from the State wherein he finds himself. And as compared with the relation of the citizen to the nation-state, the relation in the family is closer, and therefore the recognition of the service is more keenly felt by the other members.

The other objection is that under the beneficent protection of a large house there may be fostered a habit of dependence and pauperism. This objection is more substantial. But the tendency towards such a defect may be remedied by internal regulation ; such as proportionate appropriation, or mere nominal reward for the more valuable service rendered ; or differentiated rights over the disposition of the family fortune; or special privilege for the distinguished members in representing the family, etc. A definite scheme the families will devise for themselves. Such internal distinction in favour of the talented or active members would give impetus to ambition and self-development, and make pauperization less probable.

However, in the relation between husband and wife, even such distinction is not to be recommended; for they have become *one* personality. The married woman may assert herself by promoting the well-being of the family and by using its advantages. Whether the common fortune is spent under the name of the husband or the wife, makes no difference. The matter must be left to be determined by the custom of the community.[1] The essential thing is that in disposing of any portion of the common fortune, the proposals of either party must have the approval of the other. A possible objection to this is that to require such a concurrence may restrict the freedom of both. But to the writer's mind, if the proposal of either party be reasonable, the other is not likely to refuse, seeing that they have become one person. On the other hand, if the proposal of either party is not reasonable enough to secure the concurrence of the other, such freedom of extreme individualism ought to be restricted instead of being indulged, in the interest of the common good of the family. In any case a distinction of property between husband and wife is unwholesome. Should they not be able to agree with one another, there is no reason to retain a formal union of such uncongenial elements. Distinction tends to disintegrate the united personality and to make the two individuals implicitly assume an external attitude towards each other, and even to act in complete independence of each other. In other words, a state of mutual indifference or antagonism is very likely to develop, notwithstanding that such a state of mind is contradictory to the purpose of marriage.

Besides the basis of a substantial reality—the family fortune or property—the family also needs a basis of spiritual reality, that is, a well-founded tradition of the family spirit as signified by the *Penates*

---

1. For instance, in some communities, charity and similar activities distinctly belong to woman.

and other figurative expressions. The latter is even more essential to the existence of the family and worthy of being maintained and handed down to posterity than the former. For the latter is concerned with the end of the family whereas the former pertains only to the means.

The *Penates* are the Universal and Eternal Spirit as appropriated and preserved by the family, just as *Athene* is the Universal and Eternal Spirit appropriated and preserved by the nation. They both have a right to receive reverence; for they perform functions necessary to the whole process of realizing the Universal Spirit. It is observable in ordinary experience that the individuals coming from a family with well-founded moral traditions or from a nation with an advanced *ethos*, are more susceptible of higher aims and have better taste and greater aptitude to cultural development than those coming from the contrasted families and nations, although they all are under the same atmosphere of Universal Spirit. The reason for this is not far to seek. The *Penates* and *Athene* are more intimate, and so more warm to the House and the Nation than the *general* Universal Spirit is to them. Hence the former are more stimulating and accessible for the individuals to aspire to and appropriate ; and so, are more effective in instilling or rather transmitting the Universal Spirit than the Universal Spirit itself. Of course, both the *Penates* and *Athene* are particular and limited, and so must submit themselves to a mediation through the Universal and Eternal Spirit; but without them the general Spirit itself is vague and intangible, and consequently will tend to be barren and indifferent to the individuals. In a word, the *Penates* and *Athene* are the necessary medium through which alone the Universal Spirit can be transmitted to individuals. And in this sense, the *Penates* and *Athene* may have each a secondary place beside the Universal and Eternal Spirit.

Hegel *exalted* the *Athene*, but disparaged the *Penates*. [1] This is a logical consequence of his intention to emphasize the national spirit, in view of the temporary crisis of his nation. He is also

1. See Rechtsph, sect. 257.

accused of elevating the national spirit to replace by it the Universal and Eternal. Indeed, he often slides into the national Spirit, when he is speaking of the Universal and Eternal. [1] This is not, however, peculiar to him. As a rule, any attempt to approach and represent the Universal and Eternal tends to particularize or nationalize it. There is, therefore, so far no adequate representation of the Universal and Eternal Spirit. *Jehovah* has been universalized in Christendom, but at first he was only a God of the Hebrews. According to the common practice in the henotheism of the Semitic race, he was regarded by the Hebrews as the one God before others, as the specific tribal God or lord of his peculiar people. [2] Moreover, the recognition of him as the Universal and Eternal God by the Christian nations, is perhaps only *nominal*. In point of fact, *Jehovah* as well as Christianity means one thing to one nation and another thing to another. And what is true of the different nations of Christendom is no less true of the various ages of the Christian era,—not to mention the quarrels of the sects and other minor differences. The altars of the Christian churches to-day have been invaded by national flags, and sermons have oftentimes been replaced by patriotic orations. Missionary activities too at their best are only an attempt to impose one *national* culture upon other nations,[3] if we do not, as some Western writers have done, say they are the preliminary steps of imperialism, or rather means to the political and economic exploitation of other nations.

Hegel is perfectly right in placing the *support* or rearing and the *education* of the children in charge of the family. The former should not be delegated to society or the State. Not only must the parents be responsible for what flows from their own deed (*Tat*), but the young cannot dispense with the affectionate care of their parents. Nor can the parents afford to let their young go out of their sight.

---

1. Cf. before, pp. 104–106.
2. See Otto Pfleiderer, Phil. of Religion, Vol. III, pp. 117–119.
3. See the Proceedings of the American Philosophical Association, 1917.

Education, also, should not be wholly intrusted to society or to the State. Not only does public education still need the supplement of family education; but family education has a certain unique value and influence in the formation of the character of the young. There are some essentials of character-making which the individual must receive from the training of the home. If he fail to acquire them or the family fail to furnish them, he can hardly make up the defect from what is provided by public education. Hegel is, to some extent, also right in insisting upon the inheritance of the family fortune by the children rather than by any claim based upon a mere free will. For the latter is liable to be capricious.

However, Hegel failed to insist, in return, on (1) the support and care of the aged parents by the adult children; or (2) the respect, honour and glorification of the family by society and the state; or (3) the improvement of the family tradition and promotion of the family-status by its educated son or sons. (1) The support and the care of the aged parents by the mature children is very essential. Not only should there be a relation of give-and-take between parents and children; but the parents cannot dispense with the devoted care, pious consolation, filial reverence and earnest service of the children, and still less with the happiness of association with the children and the feeling of presiding over a large and flourishing family. Nor can children of good disposition bear to leave their parents miserable, lonely, melancholy, ill-treated, or neglected. State pensions for the old can solve the problem of material subsistence only, but can do nothing on the spiritual side of the problem. They cannot, for example, satisfy the longing for an intimacy of *spirit with spirit* between parents and children. Moreover, a State-pension has practical inconveniences as compared with direct support and service by the children themselves. These things, then, are better done by the family; usually the State has no good reason to intervene. What is true of the rearing and primary education of the children is no less true of the support and care of the aged parents. Should the mature children be in need of pecuniary aid because they have the further burden of their own young ones, the State or society may offer it but not take over the filial responsibility. Hegel, like many Western thinkers lets the State do too much. This common bias of the West is due to the influence of Greek civilization, which unduly emphasized the State almost to the exclusion of other social institutions.

However (2) society and the State can and should do something for the family. Society must respect and honour the family from whose son or sons some good benefit has been received or is expected. The state must reward and glorify the family whose members have rendered valuable service to the nation. Society exists for the family in the sense that it furnishes the medium and gives incentive to the development of the family, and accords recognition and gratitude for service rendered. The State exists for the family in the sense that it not only protects the family, but also encourages its prosperity and rewards its performances. The family, on the other hand, exists for both society and the State, for it can make itself respected, honoured, glorified, only in so far as it produces persons who can serve and contribute to the life of society and the state. Discrimination by society and the state may be said to be undemocratic. But democracy can carry only equality of opportunity for all; it should not refuse distinction for final attainment to special individuals. If it should abolish all sorts of distinction it could hope to attain only the darkness of a night wherein all sheep are black.

There are communities in the world where the children are not held responsible for the support and care of the parents. Nor is the parent respected, honoured, glorified, by society and the State simply because he or she has brought up and educated brilliant children. Respect, honour, etc., are obtained only by personal achievement, and an easy (not to say happy) life in old age can be secured only by accumulation of money in earlier years. The result [1] has been an outcry against the slavery

---

1. For the rest of the paragraph, see J. Tufts, Ethics of Family; International Jour. of Ethics, 1916; B. Russell, Marriage and Population Question; *Ibid.;* and similar articles in the same Journal and in the Survey.

and irksomensss of rearing and educating children, and this dissatisfaction has too often been followed by a disposition not to have children. If they come without intention, their education is likely to be neglected. Some couples deliberately choose to bring up one child, and one only. This, however, is not because they recognize their doing so as the imperative duty of all mankind, but simply because they wish to experience the interest and possible joy of having a child. The practice can, of course, be traced to many causes; but the lack of gratitude, in the internal life of the family, or in the social life *outside* of it, may be an important one.

(3) The improvement of the family tradition and the promotion of the family status by its educated son or sons are also important. The spirit of the House is after all limited. It has to be improved by drawing some new elements from the spirit of the nation, and above all from the Universal and Eternal Spirit; and to do this for the family is the principal task of its educated sons. Similarly the promotion of the family standing is to be emphasized. This can be effected by changes of occupation. For instance, when a family becomes financially prosperous, lucrative or money-making, work should be regarded as wanting in progressiveness, while literary activities and artistic pursuit, scientific investigation and philosophical speculations, social reformation and religious enterprise, etc., should be undertaken. This sort of work contributes greatly to the augmentation and enrichment of the content of human life. With success in these activities the social rank of the family is automatically elevated. Here we may be exposed to the charge of particularism. But, as a matter of fact, the progress of the nation must be accomplished through families which have produced commanding personalities. What is true of the progress of the nation is also true of that of the world. It is a pity that the children of wealthy but uncultivated families are liable to be left undeveloped; for being assured of a comfortable life, they lack understanding and appreciation of what is spiritual, intellectual, moral, etc. Such persons are social parasites and detrimental both to the family and to society at large. State regulations directed against such persons would be an

infringement of individual liberty. But public opinion, which looks down upon such persons, would form an unofficial remedy.

Hegel's conception of society is too narrow. It is concerned only with the "business" aspect of life and what follows from or is presupposed by it. Literary union, artistic brotherhood, scientific co-operation, etc., are not provided for, and pure friendship is even expressly opposed in the discussion of the inheritance of family fortune. Corporations or Trade-Societies exist largely for material efficiency. Yet Hegel is right in asserting that the aspect of *Bourgeois* society, with the form of consciousness belonging to it, is necessary to a modern State. This is in accordance with his metaphysical position that every true whole shall have aspects of difference, or should break up into particulars. He saw that this aspect of life needs some juristic adjustment. Hence the provision of the Administration of Justice. But this function properly belongs to the State instead of to civic Society. That shows that Society and State cannot be too sharply demarcated. His proposal for a State-regulation and inspection of goods offered to the public, and of the manner of consumption, is to be commended, while his advocacy of provision and undertaking by public agency has anticipated the later State-socialism which in principle is unobjectionable. The only question is how to carry out such work effectively and conveniently, if Society takes over too much from the side of individuals.

Hegel is right in asserting that the organization of the State is the realization of freedom; that is to say, the actualization of the spirit of the nation *(Volksgeist)*. To him, a nation with no State system is still in the condition of savagery.[1] The reason is that in order to realize the spirit of a nation, the nation must take definite steps to organize its own spirit into definite form. However, the form is after all only instrumental, no matter how important an instrument it be. To be more specific, the formation of a State is only a means to the end of the full development and free expression of the nation. Of course, Hegel was confronted by a situation — the lack of State organization in

1. See Encycl., sect. 549.

Germany — where form was greatly needed. Inevitably, then, he over-emphasized form, forgetting that it is only a means to the end. Nay, he. even, perhaps unintentionally, reversed the objects of means and end. In one passage he says, "In the existence of a nation the substantial aim is to be a state and preserve it as such." [1] The better form for his statement is perhaps that in the existence of a nation the substantial aim is to be a nation and preserve it as such, but as this can be done only by the formation of the nation into a state, the organization of the state is a paramount necessity to the very being of the nation.

At any rate, Hegel's view of the State is greatly distorted by the conditions of his time. His discussion is quite dominated by interest in the formal and instrumental; while the unitary spirit, on which the formation of a state must depend, is generally neglected if not quite out of sight. Hegel's discussion, therefore, seems to mean that the government is the state. And by government he logically means the organic totality of the legislature, the executive and the judiciary. But sometimes, he means only the administrative power (executive and judiciary), that is to say, a hierarchy of civil service headed, as he insisted, by the monarch.[2] Professor Reyburn [3] has pointed out the inconsistency of Hegel's discussion concerning these points in his Encyclopædia and Philosophy of Right, and has admirably refuted his insistence upon the institution of Monarchy, and, above all, his identification of Sovereignty with a Monarch. He quotes, as an account of Hegel's favour and bias towards Monarchy, what Ranke said of Bacon : "He loved the Monarchy because he expected great things from it." This is interesting and also true. At any rate, Hegel's view of the state is too official. Aristotle maintains that the constitution, i.e., the organized spirit of the group, is the State. From the ethical standpoint, the view of this ancient philosopher has probably not yet been surpassed by his modern successors.

---

1. Encycl., sect. 549.
2. See Encycl., section 541 and Phil. of Right, sect. 273.
3 See his Hegel's Ethical Theory, pp. 241–52.

But Hegel presents to us a very sound conception of a constitution.[1] To him, a constitution as well as a civil code never was made, in the ordinary sense of "law-making." It is a development from the national spirit and advances in a parallel process with that spirit's own development, running with this spirit through the same grades of formation and the alternations required by its conception. In other words, what makes the constitution is the indwelling spirit and the history of the nation, which is only the history of its spirit. To ask : To whom belongs the power to make a constitution ? is the same as to ask : Who makes the spirit of a nation ? [2] In this connection, Hegel also rightly lays it down that the guarantee of a constitution lies in the collective spirit of the nation, and also in the actual organization or development of it into suitable institutions.

Hegel's proposal that representation should be based upon differences of social groups instead of geographical differences is well worth consideration.[3] An unorganized mass cannot elect a real representative, for its members have no common interest, no common view of life, and so nothing definite to be represented. It has oftentimes been complained that the representative, when once elected, turns out to be a parliamentary tyrant, that is to say, does not represent the constituency which elected him. But, in fact, this is not the fault of the representative, He cannot help it, for the constituency has no common quality and no definite shape so that he can be instructed from time to time. A democracy based merely on geographical representation inevitably becomes a plutocratic oligarchy. At present, the representation of the Soviet is professedly based on social groups.[4] Yet it has not proved successful, for it is involved with communism ; and at the same time, the social groups of that country are lacking in adequate organization. At any rate, the

---

1. See Encycl., sect. 540.
2. See before, pp. 66-67.
3. See before, pp. 67-68.
4. The British Parliament has members from social groups, but is not principally composed of such members. The American Senator has to receive instruction from his constituency, but this is again a geographical unit.

principle of representation is not to blame. Hegel's insistence upon the co-ordination of the several branches of government and their final unity by means of the head of the State,—in place of a separation of powers, is quite right, but rather commonplace. However, he is to be credited with pointing out that the strength of a country lies neither in the multitude of its inhabitants and fighting men, nor in its fertility, nor in its size, but solely in the way its parts are by reasonable combination made into a single force which enables everything to be used for the common cause.

In regard to International Polity we find little instruction in Hegel. He lived at a time when the independence and sovereignty of States was overwhelmingly predominant ; relations between them are a secondary thing. So, inevitably, he laid too much stress on the individuality of the State, so as to make it almost a Monad, exclusive of other similar Monads. He realizes that a state must be related to other states for its completion, and that a higher ethical relationship ought to be formed between the various states. But, to him, any relation which has binding force involves an encroachment on the freedom of the nation, no matter whether it be self-formed or not. Again, he realizes that Universal History is not an efficient judgement of the world. An effective expression, nay, pronouncement of the ethical relationship of the several states requires the provision of an authority which can decide against the State and enforce its decision. This Hegel could never admit. So he left the problem where it was.

In the discussion of Universal History,[1] however, Hegel acknowledged that the independence of the restricted spirit of a nation is something secondary. It must submit to the Dialectic of the various national spirits. Again, the spirits of the nations are the stages and steps of the movement of the liberation of the Spiritual Substance. Each of these Spirits is appointed to occupy only one grade and accomplish one task in the whole process. And even the nation in which the Universal Spirit for the time invests its will, must be finally delivered over to

1. See before, p. 69.

change and decay. But when he set to work out his " Philosophy of History," he took the Germanic world for the maturity and final development of the Spiritual Substance. This virtually amounts to saying that the Universal Spirit has passed all its possible stages and hence is destined to die soon. One may agree or disagree with him as to whether the Germanic world is really more advanced in every way. But, at any rate, I do not think anybody will agree that the Universal Spirit has reached its final stage and is near its death. Again, his view of the relation between Art, Religion and Philosophy is unacceptable. According to him, the day of Art is past, and Religion finds its true expression and statement only in Philosophy. In other words, beauty and good ness are submerged in truth. This is another instance of his misapplication of the Dialectic, i.e., his way of taking distinct concrete concepts as the opposing abstractions.

Hegel's discussion of other points concerning Ethics is worth noting, but, as has been hinted, an exhaustive examination of them is not within the plan of this treatise. In conclusion it may be said that in principle he is generally right, except for a slight bias towards intellectualism and some inconsiderate use of his Dialectic. But as to specific points he is over-influenced by the contemporary situation and also limited by the state of knowledge in his day. Yet, on the whole, we owe him as much as a single thinker could ever hope to contribute.

英文現代中國教育行政

RECONSTRUCTION OF MODERN
EDUCATIONAL ORGANIZATIONS IN CHINA

By Chiling Yin, Ph.D.

Professor of Education, Shanghai College of Commerce

Pp. xviii+171. $1.20

This book is Dr. Yin's dissertation for his Ph.D. degree in New York University, and contains information regarding educational conditions in China down to 1923. The author pays special attention to considering the reorganization in the control of modern Chinese education. It supplements Dr. P. W. Kuo's excellent book entitled "The Chinese System of Public Education," which ended in 1924.

Part I of this book deals with the general organization of the different agencies of educational control in China since the establishment of the modern system of education. It shows the relation of the historical changes and the present practice of educational control. Part II reviews the movements for reorganization, with special reference to provincial and local districts. At the end the author gives his views and recommendations as to what ought to be the permanent organization of educational agencies under the Chinese Republic.

Several charts help to visualize the relation of the different departments of education in China. Persons who are interested in education will find this book most helpful as a work of reference or a textbook for classes. It is an important contribution to the literature on China written in the English language.

THE COMMERCIAL PRESS, LIMITED, PUBLISHERS

英 文 人 生 理 想 之 比 較 研 究

A COMPARATIVE STUDY OF
LIFE IDEALS

BY YU-LAN FUNG, B.A., PH.D.

In English, pp. 264+xii. Cloth, $1.80

THE author of this book has spent many years in studying Chinese and Western philosophy, first in the National University of Peking under prominent Chinese teachers, then in the Graduate School of Columbia University, New York, under Professor Dewey and Dean Woodbridge. In this book, which was written under the guidance of Professor Dewey, the author has presented the various philosophical views of human life and its ideals both Oriental and Occidental.

The book is divided into three parts, the first two parts treating of what the author calls the Ways of Decrease and Increase as evidenced in the idealization of nature and of art, and the last part treating of the continuity of art and nature and of the good of activity. The different great thinkers of ancient and modern times, of the East and the West, such as Chuang-tze, Plato, Schopenhauer, Confucius, Aristotle, to mention only a few, are thus brought face to face in a general discussion regarding the all-important question of the meaning and goal of human life, in a way that is both instructive and entertaining.

Although the book is of a philosophical nature, yet it is not without interest to ordinary readers, as it is written in a simple and straightforward style and does not contain too many technical terms. But to students of philosophy the book is invaluable, as it will help a good deal towards understanding the true relation between Eastern and Western philosophical thoughts with regard to one of the most central philosophical problems.

THE COMMERCIAL PRESS, LIMITED, PUBLISHERS
F140

國 際 上 之 中 國

CHINA IN THE FAMILY OF NATIONS

By Henry T. Hodgkin, M. A., M. B.   5″ × 7½″

Pp. 367.   Special Edition for the Far East

$3.00 Mex.

Dr. Hodgkin has been a student of China and the Chinese for more than twenty years, during which time he lived in Szechwan and traveled extensively throughout the Far East.   At present he is a secretary of the National Christian Council of China.   Thus he has had varied experience and intimate knowledge of China.

This volume contains eleven lectures given at the Selly Oak Colleges.   It gives a brief survey of the historical setting necessary for an understanding of China's present relations with the West ; it explains and estimates the various forces now working in China, producing changes in the political, social, industrial, and intellectual spheres ; it supplies a point of view which may help the reader in further study or as he watches the unfolding drama.

The author is noted for his internationalism and he looks at the problems of China in a sympathetic spirit.   He attempts to show the results of the closer contact of China with the rest of the world and what this means for China and mankind.   He discusses the international situation, the industrial development of China, and the New Thought Movement.   While the dangers are frankly faced, emphasis is laid on the possibility of good for China and for the whole family of nations.   His viewpoint is very different from the cocksureness and impatience of most foreigners who write on China, and will help to correct the distorted ideas concerning China in many books published in the English language and in magazines.

THE COMMERCIAL PRESS, LIMITED, DISTRIBUTORS

F 130